BREATHTURN

Paul Celan

BREATHTURN

*Translated from the German
and with an Introduction by
Pierre Joris*

SUN &
MOON

CLASSICS

74

SUN & MOON PRESS
LOS ANGELES • 1995

Sun & Moon Press
A Program of The Contemporary Arts Educational Project, Inc.
a nonprofit corporation
6026 Wilshire Boulevard, Los Angeles, California 90036

This edition first published in 1995 by Sun & Moon Press
10 9 8 7 6 5 4 3 2 1
FIRST ENGLISH LANGUAGE EDITION
© Suhrkamp Verlag Frankfurt am Main, 1967
English language translation ©1995 by Pierre Joris
Introduction ©1995 by Pierre Joris
Published in German as *Atemwende* by Suhrkamp Verlag
(Frankfurt am Main, 1967).
Reprinted by permission of Suhrkamp Verlag.
Biographical material ©1995 by Sun & Moon Press

This book was made possible, in part, through an operational grant from
the Andrew W. Mellon Foundation and through contributions to
The Contemporary Arts Educational Project, Inc.,
a nonprofit corporation

Cover: Alejandro Fogel, *Scratches in the train I*
Design: Katie Messborn
Typography: Guy Bennett

LIBRARY OF CONGRESS CATALOGING IN PUBLICATION DATA
Celan, Paul [1920–1970]
Breathturn
p. cm—(Sun & Moon Classics: 74)
ISBN: 1-55713-217-8 [hardcover edition]
ISBN: 1-55713-218-6 [trade paperback edition]
I. Title. II. Series. III. Translator
811'.54—dc20

Printed in the United States of America on acid-free paper.

CONTENTS

INTRODUCTION

1. "Death is a master from Germany"

Since his death in 1970, Paul Celan's reputation, though already firmly established while he was alive, has grown exponentially. George Steiner's assessment that "Celan is almost certainly the major European poet of the period after 1945," has proved accurate. Only Rilke, among this century's German-language poets, can conceivably match his fame and impact on German and world poetry. Despite the difficulties the work presents (or maybe because of them) the usual post-mortem eclipse, so often visited upon poets well-known and influential during their lifetime, did not touch Celan; the flow of essays, commentaries and books has not only continued unabated, but has picked up speed and grown to flood-tide proportions—more than 3000 items by now! A touchstone of limit-possibilities for many younger poets both in Europe and America, Celan's work has also proved a major attraction for contemporary philosophy. As Hölderlin functioned for the late Heidegger, so does Celan represent a lodestone pointing to directions "north of the future" for philosophers and writers as diverse as Otto Pöggeler, Maurice Blanchot, Jacques Derrida, Hans-Georg Gadamer, Philippe Lacoue-Labarthe and

Peter Szondi, who have all devoted at least one book to his work.

Celan's life is inseparable from the fate of the Jewish people in the Twentieth Century. The Shoah is indisputably the central event around which both the life and the work turn: he is a survivor of the Khurbn (to use Jerome Rothenberg's "ancient and dark word"), and his work is a constant bearing witness to those atrocities. Born Paul Antschel in Czernowitz, the capital of the Bukovina, in 1920, Paul Celan was raised in a Jewish family that insisted both on young Paul receiving the best secular education—with the mother inculcating her love of the German language and culture—and knowledge of his Jewish roots: both his parents came from orthodox family backgrounds, on one side Hassidic. In the summer of 1939, returning to Czernowitz after his first year as a medical student at the University of Tours in France, where he had come in contact with contemporary French literature, Celan started to write poetry and decided to study Romance literature. The next year Soviet troops occupied his home town, only to be replaced by Rumanian and German Nazi troops in 1941. Celan had to work in forced labor camps, where, in the late fall of 1942 he learned that his father, physically broken by the slave labor he was subjected to, had been killed by the ss. Later that winter the news reached him that his mother too had been shot by the Nazis. These killings, especially that of his mother, were to remain the core experience of his life. He was released a year later and remained for one more year at the now Sovietized University of Czernowitz. In April 1945 he left his hometown for good to settle in Bucharest, working as a translator and writing poetry, some of it in Rumanian. In December 1947 he clandestinely crossed over to Vienna, which in turn he left in July 1948 to settle in Paris, the city that was to be his home until his death by drowning in the Seine in late April 1970. His first major volume of poems, *Mohn und Gedächtnis*, had been published in 1952 and had brought instant recognition as well as a measure of fame, due in no small part to what was to become one of the best known and most anthologized poems of the postwar era: the "Todesfuge." A new volume of poems followed roughly every three years (with that rhythm accelerating, as we shall see, during the last years of his life). Four posthumous collections have come out, as well as two editions of "Collected Works," including all the (poetry) translations he did from a variety of languages.

2. "Lesestationen im Spätwort"

In the early sixties, i.e. midway through his writing career, a radical change, a poetic "Wende" or turn occurred, later inscribed in the title of the volume *Atemwende / Breathturn*, heralding the poetics he was to explore for the rest of his life. The poems, which had always been highly complex but rather lush with an abundance of near-surrealistic imagery and sometimes labyrinthine metaphoricity—though Celan vehemently denied the critics' suggestion that his was a "hermetic" poetry—were pared down, the syntax grew tighter and more spiny, his trademark neologisms and telescoping of words increased, while the overall composition of the work became much more "serial" in nature, i.e. rather than insisting on individual, titled poems, he moved towards a method of composition by cycles and volumes. Borrowed from a poem in another late volume, the title of this section—*Lesestationen im Spätwort*—translates as "reading stations in the late-word," which I have elsewhere described as being, for the reader, "a momentary stopping, a temporary 'station' as in the Christian deambulation of the stations of the cross, out of sheer bafflement or even despair at ever being able to grasp this work, yet also and simultaneously moments of rest, of refreshment and nourishment." Primarily, however, it indicates one of the points of entry, maybe the one most immediately visible for any reader coming to this work. Celan tells us where we have to stop and knock— or beg—for entry: in front of the word. To grasp what is at stake we have to hear what has been erased and simultaneously kept alive in the neologism "Spätwort," namely the word "Spätwerk"; to get to the "late work" we have to stop in front of the "late word," we have to come to terms with the development away from a poetry of flowing musical lines and lyric melody, as they reign supreme in the early collections, to one consisting of terse, often single-word or -syllable verse-structures, thus from a predominantly horizontal to an ever more vertiginously vertical axis. Singular words, extracted, it is true, from a vast array of rich language-veins now carry the weight of the poem. As Steiner puts it: "Such words must be quarried from far and stony places. They lodge

16

in the 'wall of the heart.'... Their authority is, in the true sense, radical, of the root (etymological). Or it springs from fusion, from the poet's right and need to weld neologisms."

Celan seems to have signaled that a change in his poetics was taking place as far back as 1958, when he suggested that for him poetry was no longer a matter of "transfiguring" (*verklären*). The statement came in a short text written as a reply to a questionnaire from the Librairie Flinker in Paris and needs quoting more fully, as it shows Celan already thinking about changes that will only be implemented in the poetry of the sixties, and which the volume *Sprachgitter*, to be published the following year, foreshadows without fully developing. Given "the sinister events in its memory" writes Celan, the language of German poetry has to become "more sober, more factual...'greyer.'" This greater factuality checks a core impulse of the lyrical tradition, its relation to the "lyre," to music: "it is... a language which wants to locate even its 'musicality' in such a way that it has nothing in common with the 'euphony' which more or less blithely continued to sound alongside the greatest horrors." An effect of giving up this "euphony" is perhaps to increase the accuracy of the language: "It does not transfigure or render 'poetical'; it names, it posits, it tries to measure the area of the given and the possible."

Celan underscores this turning point, this Wende, when he uses the word in the title of the present volume: *Atemwende/Breathturn*—an unusual title in the general economy of the naming of his books, at least until that period. Contrary to the titles of the previous volumes, it is neither a phrase, such as *Mohn und Gedächtnis,* nor a compound word extracted from a poem and set above the whole collection as title, such as *Sprachgitter.* Unable to link the title directly to a specific poem in the collection, it is difficult to determine or control its meaning by contextualizing it thematically or tropically within the book. Thus the sense that the title is programmatic for the poetics of the work rather than evoking a specific poetic content. And indeed, the word "Atemwende" does occur elsewhere in Celan's writings—namely in the Meridian speech (delivered on the occasion of receiving the Georg Büchner Prize in Darmstadt, 22 October 1960) which is his most important and extended statement on poetics. It is here that we have to look for the theoretical base of the changes from the early to late work.

In the speech, Celan addresses the question of art through the work of Georg Büchner. He defines Lucile's final exclamation "Long live the king!" as "a word against the grain, the word which cuts the 'string,' which does not bow to the 'bystanders and old warhorses of history.' It is an act of freedom. It is a step." In short it is what Celan calls a "Gegenwort," a counter-word, and thus the word of poetry. But, he goes on, there is an even fiercer "Gegenwort," and that is Lenz's silence: "Lenz—that is, Büchner—has gone a step farther than Lucile. His 'Long live the king' is no longer a word. It is a terrifying silence. It takes his—and our—breath and words away." It is in the next sentence that he introduces the term "Atemwende":

Poetry is perhaps this: an *Atemwende,* a turning of our breath. Who knows, perhaps poetry goes its way—the way of art—for the sake of just such a turn? And since the strange, the abyss and Medusa's head, the abyss *and* the automaton, all seem to lie in the same direction—is it perhaps this turn, this *Atemwende,* which can sort out the strange from the strange? It is perhaps here, in this one brief moment, that Medusa's head shrivels and the automatons run down? Perhaps, along with the I, estranged and freed *here, in this manner,* some other thing is also set free?

Perhaps after this, the poem can be itself... can in this now artless, art-free manner go other ways, including the ways of art, time and again?

Perhaps.

I have quoted this passage at length not only because it may be the one which most closely defines Celan's thinking about poetry, but also to give a sense of its rhetorical texture, its tentative, meditative, one could say groping, progress. The temptation—and many critics have not resisted it—would be to extract from the passage the definitive, affirmative statement "poetry is a breathturn," but in the process one would have discarded the whole series of rhetorical pointers, the ninefold repetition of the word "vielleicht" (the English translation uses "perhaps" only seven times) which turns all the sentences into questions. The passage is, however, not an isolated rhetorical formula in the speech; indeed, one could argue that the whole of the Meridian is a putting into question of the possibilities of art, in Celan's own words, "eine radikale In-Frage-Stellung der Kunst," which all of poetry (and art in general) has to submit to today, if it wants to be of essential use. Gerhard Buhr, in an excellent essay analyzing the Meridian speech from exactly that angle, comments on Celan's expression "eine radikale In-Frage-Stellung der Kunst" as follows:

> The phrase "radikale In-Frage-Stellung der Kunst" (radical putting-into-question of art) has a double meaning given the two ways the genitive can read: Art, with "everything that belongs and comes to it"… has to be radically questioned; and it [art] puts other things, such as man or poetry, radically into question. That is exactly why the question of poetry, the putting-into-question of poetry is not exterior to art—: The nature of art is rather to be discussed and clarified in connection with the nature of the question itself. (Buhr 1988, 171)

Celan, a careful poet not given to rhetorical statements or linguistic flourishes, who in his late poems will castigate himself and his own early work for an overuse of such "flowers," needs to be taken quite literally here: he is groping, experimenting, questioning, trying to find his way to a new possibility in poetry. It is a slow process: the term "Atemwende," coined in this speech of 1960 will reemerge as the title of a volume seven years later.

The last book published before the Meridian speech

had been *Sprachgitter,* which had come out the previous year (1959) and already points to some of the directions the late work will take. For the first time Celan uses a single, compound word as a title, something he will do for all subsequent volumes; for the first time it contains poems, albeit only five, devoid of individual titles— something that will become the norm in the late work. The language has now given up nearly completely the long dactylic lines and the rhymes of the first three books while the brief, foreshortened, often one-word, lines have become more frequent. Most importantly, some of the poems are clearly what has been called "Widerrufe": attempts at retracting, countermanding, disavowing previous poetics. The poem "Tenebrae," for example, is a carefully constructed refutation of Hölderlin's "Patmos" hymn. In a similar vein the title poem "Sprachgitter" takes issue both with Gottfried Benn's famous essay "Probleme der Lyrik," and with the optimism of Psalm 126.

However, Celan's "Widerrufe" are not only addressed to German poetry and the Scriptures. He also calls into question his own earlier poetics. One can thus read "Engführung," the great poem that concludes *Sprachgitter,* as a rewriting with different poetics of the "Todesfuge," as Hans Mayer and others have done. This critical stance towards his early poetics remains perceptible in several poems of the late work and is thematized in the opening stanza of a poem in *Breathturn:*

WEGGEBEIZT vom
Strahlenwind deiner Sprache
das bunte Gerede des An-
erlebten—das hundert-
züngige Mein-
gedicht, das Genicht.

ERODED by
the beamwind of your speech
the gaudy chatter of the pseudo-
experienced—my hundred-
tongued perjury-
poem, the noem.

The neologism "Meingedicht" is based on the German
word "Meineid," perjury, but because Celan breaks the
word the way he does, one cannot but hear in the prefix
the possessive "mein," "my." As Jerry Glenn has suggested,
this "allude[s] to Celan's own early attempts to come to
terms with the past in elaborate, colorful metaphors."
The new language of the addressed "you," which here
seems to be the poet himself, his new "beamwind"-lan-
guage aims to erode the "gaudy chatter" of the early work,
and lead into a bare northern landscape of snow and
ice: "nordwahr," "northtrue" as another poem puts it,
where the true "unalterable testimony" which it is the
poet's job to create can be found, located deep in the
ice, as an "Atemkristall," a breath-crystal.

Celan's "Widerrufe" have in common a deep dissatis-
faction with traditional (and that includes modernist)
poetics and a need to push towards a new vision of writ-

ing, the world, and the relationship between those two. For Celan, art no longer harbors the possibility of redemption in that it can neither lead back to or bring back the gods, as Hölderlin suggested, nor can it constitute itself as an independent, autonomous sphere of "Artistik" as Gottfried Benn—and behind him, the tradition that starts with Mallarmé—sees it. It is this new, experimental poetics tentatively proposed in the Meridian speech that is beginning to be implemented in the late work.

3. "Line the word-caves"

The Meridian speech thus points the way, with many "perhaps's," to the late work, but how to read these obviously difficult poems remains a problem. Happily, besides the "Widerruf" poems, Celan has written a number of programmatic meta-poems, showing how the poet envisaged the act of writing, thus how he would have liked his work to be read and understood. Let me give a somewhat detailed reading of one such poem from *Fadensonnen / Threadsuns*, the volume that follows *Breathturn*.

> KLEIDE DIE WORTHÖHLEN AUS
> mit Pantherhäuten,
>
> erweitere sie, fellhin und fellher,
> sinnhin und sinnher,

gib ihnen Vorhöfe, Kammern, Klappen
und Wildnisse, parietal,

und lausch ihrem zweiten
und jeweils zweiten und zweiten
Ton.

In my translation:

LINE THE WORD-CAVES
with panther skins,

widen them, pelt-to and pelt-fro,
sense-hither and sense-thither,

give them courtyards, chambers, drop doors
and wildnesses, parietal,

and listen for their second
and each time second and second
tone.

Following Celan's own suggestions, I have already in-
sisted on the importance of the *word* in the late poetry.
This poem thematically foregrounds the point, yielding
insights not only into Celan's writing process, but also
into the reading process. The work of poetry is to be
done on the word itself, the word that is presented here
as hollow, as a cave—an image that suggests immedi-
ately a range of connections with similar topoi through-
out the oeuvre, from prehistoric caves to Etruscan tombs.

The word is nothing solid, diorite or opaque, but a formation with its own internal complexities and crevasses—closer to a geode, to extend the petrological imagery so predominant in the work from *Breathturn* on. In the context of this first stanza, however, the "panther skins" seem to point more towards the image of a prehistoric cave, at least temporarily, for the later stanzas retroactively change this reading, giving the poem the multi-perspectivity so pervasive in the late work.

These words need to be worked on, to be transformed, enriched, in order to become meaningful. In this case the poem commands the poet to "line" them with animal skins, suggesting that something usually considered as an external covering is brought inside and turned inside-out. The geometry of this inversion makes for an ambiguous space, like that of a Klein bottle where inside and outside become indeterminable or interchangeable. These skins, pelts or furs also seem to be situated *between* something, to constitute a border of some sort, for the next stanza asks for the caves to be enlarged in at least two, if not four directions, i.e. "pelt-to and pelt-fro, / sense-hither and sense-thither." This condition of being between is indeed inscribed in the animal chosen by Celan, via a multilingual pun (though he wrote in German, Celan lived in a French-speaking environment while translating from half a dozen languages he mastered perfectly): "between" is "entre" in French, while the homophonic rhyme-word "antre" means a cave; this "antre" or cave is inscribed and can be heard in the animal name "Panther." (One could of course pursue the panther-image in other directions, for example into

Rilke's poem—and Celan's close involvement with Rilke's work is well documented.) Unhappily, the English verb "lined" is not able to render the further play on words rooted in the ambiguity of the German "auskleiden," which means both to line or dress and undress.

These "Worthöhlen," in a further echo of inversion, invoke the expression "hohle Worte"—empty words. Words, and language as such, have been debased, emptied of meaning—a topos that can be found throughout Celan's work—and in order to be made useful again the poet has to transform and rebuild them, creating in the process those multiperspectival layers that constitute the gradual, hesitating yet unrelenting mapping of Celan's universe. The third stanza thus adds a further stratum to the concept of "Worthöhlen" by introducing physiological terminology, linking the word-caves to the hollow organ that is the heart. These physiological topoi appear with great frequency in the late books and have been analyzed in some detail by James Lyon, who points out both the transfer of anatomical concepts and terminology, and, specifically in this poem, how the heart's atria become the poem's courtyards, the ventricles, chambers and the valves, drop doors. The poem's "you," as behooves a programmatic text, is the poet exhorting himself to widen the possibilities of writing by adding attributes, by enriching the original word-caves. The poem's command now widens the field by including "wildnesses," a term that recalls and links back up with the wild animal skins of the first stanza. Celan does not want a linear transformation of the word from one singular meaning to the next, but he strives for the constant presence of the multiple layers of meaning accreting in the process of the poem's composition. The appearance in the third stanza of these wildnesses also helps to keep alive the tension between a known, ordered, constructed world and the unknown and unexplored, which is indeed the Celanian "Grenzgelände," that marginal borderland into which, through which and from which language has to move for the poem to occur.

But it is not just a question of simply adding and enlarging, of a mere constructivist activism; the poet also has to listen. The last stanza gives this command, specifying that it is the second tone that he will hear that is important. The poem itself foregrounds "tone"; it is the last word of the poem, constituting a whole line by itself while simultaneously breaking the formal symmetry of the text which had so far been built up on stanzas of two lines each. Given the earlier heart imagery, this listening to a double tone immediately evokes the systole / diastole movement. The systole corresponds to the contraction of the heart muscle when the blood is pumped through the heart and into the arteries, while the diastole represents the period between two contractions of the heart when the chambers widen and fill with blood. The triple repetition on the need to listen to the second tone thus insists that the sound produced by the diastole is what is of interest to the poet.

The imagery of the heart and of the circulation of the blood is of course a near-classical topos in poetry; Celan, however, transforms it in such a way that it becomes vital poetic imagery at the end of this century. In no way is it readable as a kind of postmodernist (in the aesthetical-architectural sense) citation or pastiche of classical poetic/decorative topoi. Numerous other poems take up, develop and transform this and related imagery. Here, as one example, is a poem which appears four pages after "Line the word-caves" and which speaks of this second movement, though this time from an anatomical position slightly above, though still near the heart:

> NEAR, IN THE AORTIC ARCH,
> in the light-blood:
> the light-word.
>
> Mother Rachel
> weeps no more.
> Carried over:
> all the weepings.
>
> Quiet, in the coronary arteries,
> unconstricted:
> Ziv, that light.

The poem centers around both historical and kabbalistic Judaic motifs (*Ziv* is Hebrew for splendor and refers to the mystical light of the Shekinah), though the place it opens out from and which grounds it—"the aortic arch" of the "coronary arteries"—clearly links it to the biological/anatomical topos of "Line the word-caves." Returning briefly to the latter poem, let me close this *excursus* by presenting another, additive reading of some of the complexities in "Line the word-caves." In a brilliant essay, Werner Hamacher discusses the movement of the figure of inversion as central to the poetics of late Celan, using a poem from *Sprachgitter,* "Stimmen," and concentrating on the line "sirrt die Sekunde" [the second buzzes] which he de- and re-constructs as "diese Kunde" [this message, this conduit of information]. In a footnote, he includes a brief analysis of "Line the word-caves," which I will cite and let stand as conclusion to my own analysis, if only to show how the poly-perspectivity of a Celan poem permits multiple approaches, all of which help to shed light on the word-caves these late poems are. Having also picked up on the sound-pun of "antre," and the transference of the animal's outer layer into the word's inside, Hamacher writes:

> Here too we have an inversion of familiar ideas.... Sense is only one—and indeed an alien, second—skin, an inner mask. Tone, as "that which is always second," is in each case distanced further than the audible tone, infinitely secondary; it too a second. Celan's later poems are written out of this second and for its sake; they are *dated,* as finite language, on the second. The inversion of the secondary into the "primary," of the outer into the "inner" is always effected in them so that they expand the character of the secondary, in *fine,* instead of domesticating it. Thus, as he himself stressed, we can only "understand" his texts "from a distance." (....) In addition, *auskleiden* is one of the possible mean-

ings of *auslegen* (to interpret). Insofar as the poem takes on this—second—sense in the image, in the clothing, in the pelt, it itself practices the hermeneutic operation it recommends: the whole becomes feline, *fellhin und fellher*, although not without falling into what would count as failure for a normative understanding.

For Hamacher, the tropes and images of Celan's poetry are thus "not metaphors for representations but metaphors for metaphorization, not images of a world but images of the generation of images, not the transcription of voices but the production of the etched voices of the poem itself."

4. "…every poem is marked by its own '20th of January.'"

The concept of "dated" poems is, however, not just a useful and elegant way of thinking theoretically through the temporal dimension of Celan's polyverse. In a very practical sense we have to be mindful of the dates of the poems in the compositional procedure of the late work— especially as Celan has carefully erased them from the books as such—if we want to understand the cyclical nature of these books. This serial mode of composition suggests the need, neglected until now, of publishing translations of the exact and complete volumes Celan himself had published—or, as far as the posthumous work goes, readied for publication—rather than excerpting a few "translatable" poems from this or that book.

An examination of early versions or publications of some of the poems in the late work show that Celan would often have a (working) title for a given poem that would be omitted later, when the poem became part of a cycle or volume. Also, it seems that all his worksheets were dated, so that a critical edition will eventually permit us to analyze in more detail the chronological construction of these late volumes and determine the grounds—chronological or other—they were built on. We do know some of their compositional history—and what we know so far tends to corroborate our intuition that these volumes were composed in the main part chronologically with a prevailing sense of serial / cyclical composition as core structuring device.

As to the volume at hand, we have in fact very specific information concerning at least some of the cycles. Otto Pöggeler, for example, tells us that Celan started work on the first cycle of *Breathturn* in the fall of 1963, shortly after the volume *Die Niemandsrose* had been printed. His research shows that the first four poems of the first cycle are dated October 16, with more poems written in the next few days. "Whitegray" is dated October 25; "Templeclamps," November 8; "In the serpentcoach," December 16; "Wordaccretion," December 24. "Eroded," the final poem in the cycle, was written on December 30. Pöggeler goes on to say: "Only the poem 'I know you,' which functions somewhat as a dedication, follows later, on January 9, 1964; this poem—and it is the only divergence in the printed sequence from the chronology of the composition—is inserted before the final poem."

We do not as yet have as precise knowledge generally available concerning the other cycles of *Breathturn*; we do, however, have tantalizing hints that they too were composed in a similar, mainly chronological and daily writing fashion. Thus Jean Bollack, who knew Celan well, writes: "Their composition is each time conceived as an instant of life, plenitude or emptiness, the instant of the act of writing (that is the only parousia, his—of a word: his) [... instant de l'écriture en acte (c'est l'unique parousie, la sienne—d'un verbe: le sien)]; the texts give themselves as such, present themselves more and more in that biographical form, like poetic notes inscribed in an open 'journal'; it opens and continues in discontinuity."

Although we can thus deduce that Celan's late work is composed more or less chronologically, different cycles are "durchkomponiert," to use a musical analogy, so as to create larger coherences. This has been shown only for a few cycles, especially the one most attentively studied until now, "Atemkristall/Breathcrystal," comprising the twenty-one poems that open *Breathturn*. This is important in that it helps us understand the serial/cyclical nature of late Celan—which in turn will play a central role in how one approaches the translation of those books, as well as being essential to any serious hermeneutical or theoretical reading of the work.

Such research and textual clarification concerning the sequence of books starting with *Breathturn* will also help dispel any notion of a "Verstummen," a falling silent by the poet, which has been one of the alibis used to dismiss the admittedly very difficult late work. Celan, or so this fallacious argument goes, in the last several years of his life, due to illness or some other unexplained cause, had either nothing left to say, or only incoherencies, as is obvious from the poems growing smaller and more gnarled and incomprehensible. This dismissive argument even attempts to bring to bear the man's suicide as alleged proof of his desperate rush towards a "Verstummen," a "becoming mute."

A quick accounting will tell us that it is not so. From the late forties until the early sixties, Celan published five collections of poems, the publication of each volume separated by roughly four years. With *Breathturn* this pattern changes drastically: the volume appears in 1967. It is the biggest single volume, containing 78 poems, while the average number of poems in the previous collections was less than fifty. *Fadensonnen/ Threadsuns* follows in rapid succession: it is published in 1968, while *Lichtzwang/Lightduress* appears in the spring of 1970, shortly after the poet's suicide. *Schneepart*, which appears in 1971, contains poems written in 1967 and 1968, thus, according to Glenn, "before those contained in *Lichtzwang* and presumably at the same time as, or shortly after, those in *Fadensonnen*." During 1967 and 1968 Celan also published two limited editions of poems that were to be gathered in *Lightduress*, and four volumes of poetry translations. To talk of "Verstummen" in the case of such high, not to say hectic, productivity is simply nonsense—or an attempt at out-of-hand dismissal; it is a reading based on critics comparing the size and word count of individual poems and speaks more to their own bafflement in the face of Celan's poetry than to the actual facts. Rather than falling silent, Celan became truly voluble in the last years of his life.

5. "Poetry is by necessity a unique instance of language."

So much so is poetry unique, that a number of practitioners and commentators have concluded it to be untranslatable. Celan's work, given its supposed and much vaunted hermeticism, given the actual and undeniable linguistic and hermeneutic difficulties it presents, has often been held up as exemplary of just such untranslatability. And yet, Celan's own practice, including as it does an immense *œuvre* of translation of very difficult poetry from half a dozen languages, certainly intimates nothing of the kind. I too—obviously—believe in the possibility of translation, would even call it a necessity, though such belief is at times sorely put to the test. Questioning the possibility of translation means to question the very possibility of literature, of writing, of language, which is always already a translation, i.e. is both an act of translation and the result of such an act. In my years spent in the practice of poetry, both writing and translating it, a sense has gropingly emerged suggesting that a poem is not only the one version printed in a book or magazine, but is also all its other (possible) printed versions, plus all the possible oral and/or visual performances as well as the totality of translations it allows. The printed poem thus functions only as score for all subsequent readings (private or public) and performative transformations, be they through music, dance, painting or linguistic translation. Such a view is bound to destabilize a concept of the poem as fixed, absolute artifact, readable (understandable, interpretable) once and for all. Celan says as much in the Meridian: "The absolute poem—no, it certainly does not, cannot exist."

I started translating *Atemwende* in 1967, the year of its publication. I did so not with the immediate intention of having it published (though I certainly did not want to exclude that possibility, even then), but rather as the only way I saw of entering into an apprenticeship with the poet to whose work I owed what I can only describe as the epiphanic experience which, six years earlier, had opened the realm of poetry as a place of life's possible quest and fulfillment. The very idea of trying to meet Celan seemed completely out of the realm of possibility at that time, despite the fact that we lived in the same city. Even if I had been less shy and awkward and had attempted to meet him, it would probably not have happened or only as disaster, given my own ignorance of poetry and the world, and Paul Celan's intensity during those last years of his life—an intensity that, I believe, wouldn't have suffered young fools gladly. There is a further reason: by 1967 I had been writing poetry in English for a mere three years, was thus very tentative and explorative in that language, and had just decided to move to the us, leaving behind a Europe I did not want to have any truck with anymore. As if we could ever leave anything behind.

In the spring of 1969 I completed the first translation

of *Breathturn* in the context of my senior project at Bard College where I had the subtle and immensely enriching advice of Robert Kelly to help me along the way. Four or five years later—by then I was living in London—Asa Benveniste, the poet and publisher of Trigram Press, proposed to print *Breathturn*. I revised the book carefully, but despite all his efforts Asa was unable to secure the rights from the German publishers and the project came to nothing. Between 1976 and 1979, living in Constantine, Algeria—and with much free time on my hands—I went yet again over the translations while starting work on *Threadsuns* and *Lightduress*. Upon my return to London—and even more so after moving to Paris in the early eighties—I became friends with Gisèle Celan-Lestrange, the poet's widow, to whom the novelist Didier Pemerle and Martine Broda, poet and French Celan translator, had introduced me in the late seventies. This friendship was a further spur that kept me working on Celan, reading, rereading, thinking and writing on the work—when I was not translating. When I moved back to the US in 1987, I brought along a near complete translation of all of late Celan, starting with *Breathturn*. Between 1988 and 1991, I reworked all of these translations yet again for a dissertation at SUNY Binghamton—an occasion that gave me the leisure and ability to catch up on the vast amount of secondary Celan literature that had accrued over the years. Much of this work proved helpful in revising and fine-tuning the translations—something I keep doing today and will no doubt keep doing in the future.

The detailed narrative of the various stages of this project is not meant to propose the count of years and the accumulation of versions as proof of quality; to the contrary: it is meant to relativize the very notion of a definitive, final translation. Any given stage was as definite a translation as I could make at that time, and next year's version would no doubt be different from this one. (On the ontogenetic level, this tale of successive versions of translations repeats the phylogenetic need for all great poems—and maybe the less great need this even more so—to be retranslated, generation after generation, to be of use. The accumulation of these readings, for that is what translations are, constitutes the [after]life of a poem.) The presentation of the Celan translations (and of most other such work of *metaphorein* I've done) that I would prefer has always been linked to the time I studied medicine: namely, to those wonderful textbook inserts consisting of a series of plastic sheets, each of which had a part or layer of the human anatomy printed on it, making for a palimpsest one could leaf through backwards and forwards. All books of translations should be such palimpsests, for if there can be a definite original text—which we know is not true, though it may be a necessary fiction from the translator's perspective—there can only be layers upon layers of unstable, shifting, tentative, other-languaged versions. But this synchronic or symphonic presentation of the versions is not a practical possibility; we will have to do with the tale of the diachrony of the work and hope that the narrative of the process will permit these versions to be seen as just that: versions, momentary stoppings and configurations in an unending process of transmutation.

There are specific problems that make translating Celan a difficult undertaking. Among them is the extremely complex, not to say complicated, relationship Celan had to the language in which he wrote. His German strongly distances itself from any use that language was put to, both in literature and as vehicle for spoken communication, either before or during the poet's lifetime. It is truly an invented German. A translator thus first has to locate the language, or rather the languages, from which Celan has "translated" his poetry into German. The sources are manifold, and commentators have laid some of these bare; to "cleanse" his language "of historical political dirt" (Steiner), Celan has often gone to earlier forms of German, so that medieval or late medieval words and etymologies enter the poems and need to be tracked down. Similarly, words no longer in current use or known only to dialectical speakers (such as North- and South-German, Austrian), make frequent appearances, baffling even native German speakers. Celan was an assiduous reader and user of Grimm's dictionary, which is probably the most important reference book for coming to terms with his language.

Celan has also mined other politically uncontaminated vocabularies (uncontaminated at least by the plague of thirties and forties Germany), such as those of botany, ornithology and entomology, but also geology, mineralogy, geography, chemistry, crystallography, nuclear physics, current and space-age technology, hunting, anatomy, physiology and medicine, with the latter gaining in importance in the late work, as James Lyon has shown. But even the ability to determine the origin of a given word rarely resolves the translator's problem. In German most of the technical and scientific terms are composite forms of common German words; in Celan's use of the terms those common word-roots shine through and create multiple levels of meaning. In English such vocabularies are mainly based on Greek or Latin roots, which severs their use from any "common" connection with the language, reducing the multi-level play of meanings. An example of a German composite term, a traditional technological description of a machine, can be found in the poem "Harbor." In the expression, "Laufkatze Leben," Celan clearly wants the reader to hear the compound word made up from the words "Katze" (cat) and "Lauf" (run) as descriptive of "Leben" (life), but the word "Laufkatze" is also, and unavoidably in the poem's harbor-geography, the technical apparatus called in English a "trolley" or "trolley hoist." Unable to find an English equivalent that would render this meaning-complex in a satisfactory manner, I have, in this particular instance, tried to play with a paratactic juxtaposition of both meanings, combined with the use of the pronoun "she" rather than the expected "it."

To complicate matters further, Celan often creates neologisms based on analogical word constructions, in which it is essential to hear (or see) the original word. Maybe the best known one—because the philosopher Hans-Georg Gadamer gave a far-fetched and hotly contested metaphorical interpretation of it—is the word "Schläfenzangen" (temple-tongs or -clamps), constructed by analogy with the word "Geburtzange," (obstetric forceps), the baby's temples being indeed the place where the obstetrician tries to apply the forceps. Celan's use of non-specialized vocabulary areas, creating word-puns and -plays, also gets lost in the process of translation. In paronomastic formations such as "rauchdünn" (smoke-thin) one hears the common expression "hauchdünn" (paper-thin, literally, breath-thin); similarly one hears "Morgenrot" ("the red of dawn," literally, "morning-red") in "Morgen-Lot," (morning-sounder or -plumb)—such exempla could be extended *ad infinitum*.

Another area that informs Celan's language is that of Jewish mysticism. While he doesn't generally create new words or word combinations (though some Hebrew word and grammar usages are on occasion adapted by Celan), his interweaving of mystical themes lays further strata of meaning on some of the most common words in the language, such as "light" or "sister." The abundant use of such specialized vocabularies and their interweaving with frequent neologisms poses problems even for the native reader. Even seasoned commentators have claimed a given word as a neologism when in fact a quick look into *Grimms Wörterbuch* would have shown the word to have been a common German word, even if no longer in use. Conversely, one often comes across a word that looks and feels like a "real" German word, but when trying to trace it one realizes that it is a Celan "invention." The effect of this manipulation of vocabularies is to create a linguistic mine-field through which the reader—and à fortiori the translator—has to move with extreme care. If I have put the word "invention" between quotation marks, it is with respect to Celan's own reported claim: "At bottom my word formations are not inventions. They belong to the very oldest layers of language." This statement may be philosophically true for its author, but it does not bring philological solace to the translator.

One also has to take into account the influence of other languages as Celan's early acquisition of and familiarity with a number of these has inflected his own writing. Rumanian would be one example, though it is likely that Russian will eventually be shown to have had a more conscious influence, not the least through Celan's very strong identification with Osip Mandelstam —one commentator speaking of the "slavification" of certain grammatical moments in Celan. French, which was the language-environment Celan functioned in during the last twenty-two years of his life, has in all probability had some influence. However, little work has been done on this as yet, except for a few commentators pointing out some rather obvious homophonic occurrences. The most often-cited of these examples occurs in a poem where the German word "Neige" (decrease) sees its French homonym meaning "snow" appear as the German "Schnee" in the next line. Another concerns Celan's use of the word "Kommissur" in a poem which plays on the German meaning that refers to an anatomical aspect of the brain and on the French word "commissure des lèvres." In English the word "commissure" happily ries both meanings and for once the polysemy is not lost in the translation.

If knowledge of these and similar complexities in Celan's language have anything to tell the translator it is essentially this: Celan's language, though German on the surface, is a foreign language, even for native speakers. Although German was his mother tongue and the *Kultursprache* of his native Bukovina, it was also, and in an essential way, his *other* tongue. Celan's German is an eerie, nearly ghostly language; it is both mother-tongue, and thus firmly anchored in the realm of the dead, and a language the poet has to make up, to re-create, to re-invent, to bring back to life. One could say that Celan raids the German language—and I use the military metaphor advisedly, for there seems to me to run through Celan's life if not a desire for assault on Germany and revenge for the death of his parents (or of his mother before all), then at least a constant, unrelenting sense of being on a war footing, of being under attack and needing to counter this attack. The Celanian dynamic is, however, not simple-minded or one-directional; it involves a complex double movement—to use the terms of Empedocles—of *philotes* (love) for his mother('s tongue) and of *neikos* (strife) against her murderers who are the originators and carriers of that same tongue.

This profound alienation in relation to his writing language is the very ground upon which and against which Celan works, or, to use the Heraclitian formula: Celan is estranged from that which is most familiar. In his answer to a questionnaire sent out by the Librairie Flinker, he wrote: "Reality is not simply there, it must be searched for and won." Reality for Celan, maybe more so than for any other poet this century, was the word, was language. Radically dispossessed of any other reality he set about to create his own language—a language as absolutely exiled as he himself. To try to translate it as if it were current, commonly spoken or available German—i.e. to find a similarly current English or American "Umgangssprache"—would be to miss an essential aspect of the poetry, the linguistic under-mining and displacement that creates a multi-perspectivity mirroring and reticulating the polysemous meanings of the work.

Celan's "language," as I have tried to show, is really a number of dismantled and recreated languages. This dismantling and rewelding, this semantic and syntactical wrenching, uses as substratum a German language that offers itself relatively willingly to such linguistic surgery. Other languages do not have that flexibility, or have it to a much lesser degree. French, for example, basically does not permit such word creations and is also resistant to the syntactical wrenchings so characteristic of late Celan—which is why it has taken so long to have even approximate translations of Celan into that language. In English the telescoping of multiple words, though more available than in French, remains problematic to say the least. Noun-composita of two elements, such as "Wortwand" / "wordwall" or "Eisdorn" / "Ice-thorn" often can be rendered as such in English, while those made up of more than two root words, such as "Rundgräberschatten" / "roundgraveshadows" or "Knochenstabritzung" / "bonerodscratch" can be unwieldy and inelegant and at times need to be broken up. The major formal problems posed by Celan's verbal grafts, however, concern his play with prefixes and affixes, especially the use of spatial adverbs and prepositions. Word formations such as "weggebeizt," "weggesackt," which sound quite natural in German, or those like "auseinandergebrannt," "hinüberdunkeln," which sound clearly artificial, invented, even in German, usually cannot be rendered by an English compound word and require circumlocutions. There are a number of more complex and stranger sounding word-creations, such as "verunewigt" or "unentworden," that are so artificial in the original that they both give permission for and require similar constructions in English: "de-eternalized" or, possibly, "diseternalized" and "undebecome" try to approach the oddity of the German constructions. Many of Celan's neologisms employ verbal or adjectival root-elements that are turned into nouns. The capitalization of nouns in German helps the reader identify such formations much more easily than is possible in English. There are, finally, no hard and fast linguistic rules the translator could apply concerning these word formations. Solutions will tend to be local and dependent on context and on the eventual readability of the English term.

Even more problematic than the vocabulary, however, are certain syntactical possibilities of German lacking in English, foremost the fact that in German it is possible to have nouns preceded by complete qualifying clauses. In the late poems, many of which are made up of long single sentences, Celan makes ample use of this possibility, thereby giving the poem a structure of suspense by deferring resolution of what or who is addressed or modified until the end of the sentence. In a poem from *Breathturn*, made up of two sentences, this problem arises several times:

> ÜBER DREI im meer-
> trunkenen Schlaf
> mit Braunalgenblut
> bezifferte Brust-
> warzensteine
>
> stülp deinen sich
> von der letzten
> Regenschnur los-
> reißenden Himmel.
>
> Und laß
> deine mit dir hierher-
> gerittene Süßwassermuschel
>
> all das hinunter-
> schlürfen, bevor
> du sie ans Ohr
> eines Uhrschattens hältst,
> abends.

Standard English syntax for the first sentence (making up the first two stanzas) would suggest a fourfold reversal of Celan's construction and would read something like this: "Clap your sky which is breaking away from the last raincord over three breast-nipple stones that are ciphered with brown-algae blood in sea-drunken sleep." Trying to keep the movement of Celan's sentence alive, so that "sky" can appear as the last word in the sentence, produces the following translation:

> OVER THREE in sea-
> drunken sleep
> with brownalgae-blood
> ciphered breast-
> nipplestones
>
> clap your
> from the last
> raincord breaking
> loose sky.

There is no doubt that the twisted syntax sounds more strained in English than in German, especially that of the clause qualifying the sky in the second stanza. One could try to make the stanza more readable in English by altering the visual organization of the lines, possibly as follows:

> clap
> your from the last
> raincord breaking loose
> sky.

But this does not remove the strain completely while falsifying the dense rhythmic movement of the original.

The third stanza presents a similar though even more intractable problem. Keeping Celan's syntax would give the following translation:

> And let
> your ridden with you to this place
> freshwatermussel....

This is clearly nonsensical in English and needs to be altered so as to read something like:

> And let
> your freshwatermussel that rode
> with you to this place...

Again, any solution is bound to be local as the translator cannot rely on a generally applicable rule but has to try to reproduce, wherever possible, the movement of Celan's language, while measuring how much strain it is reasonable to impose on the target language.

But there is another major—if more general—problem facing the translator of Celan into English. It concerns what I like to call the present episteme of American poetry, i.e. the set of presuppositions, linguistic and historical, which determine to a great extent how we hear and what we recognize as "good" poetry and, by extension, good translations. This episteme, so revivifying for American poetry over the last half century, is in part inherited from such great modernists as William Carlos Williams, Ezra Pound and others, but goes back at least as far as Walt Whitman. It demands that the language of poetry be as close as possible to the spoken, colloquial language of today. As a reaction to the genteel tradition of the British poetry of the Victorian and Edwardian ages (and its American equivalents), this has meant avoiding rhetorical flourishes and most traditional "poetic" effects. In relation to translating Celan this can all too often induce the temptation for the English versions to oversimplify the original poem, by making short shrift of the oddities of the word constructions and by ironing out the twists and quirks of Celan's syntax, in a doomed attempt to make the language sound "natural." Yet the development of Celan's poetry away from the traditional metrics and rhymes still present in the early work toward a line based on different units (breath, syllable, word), is reminiscent of certain developments in American poetry—one need only think of Olson's injunctions in the "Projective Verse" essay concerning a new breath-based metrics or compare the tight vowel-leading poetics of Louis Zukofsky's poem "A" with similar attentions in Celan's work.

In my versions I have drawn on every available scrap of information I could garner concerning the poems and on whatever poetic knowledge I have been able to gather in English. My first aim has not been to create elegant, easily readable and accessible American versions of these German (under erasure) poems. The aim has been to get as much of the complexity and multi-perspectivity of Celan's work over into American, and if elegant moments or stretches of *claritas* occur, all the better. Any translation that makes a poem sound more (or even as) accessible than it is in the original has to be flawed. I have doubtlessly not achieved what Hölderlin did with his translations from the Greek—to write Greek in German, and thus to transform the German, though that must remain the aim of any translator, just as it is the aim of any poet to transform his or her language.

There are too many who have contributed in one way or another to this work over the past 27 years for me to be able to acknowledge them all here individually. May they all be thanked, because without them this project would never have come to fruition—or would have done so with a much different and poorer result. Of course it is I who am responsible for all the remaining errors.

Pierre Joris
Albany, April 1995

Resources

Celan, P. (1967). *Atemwende.* Frankfurt a. M. Suhrkamp Verlag.

Celan, P. (1983). *Gesammelte Werke in fünf Bände.* Frankfurt a. M. Suhrkamp Verlag.

Celan, P. (1986). *Collected Prose.* Translated by Rosmarie Waldrop. Manchester, Carcanet Press.

*

Bollack, J. (1987). "Pour Une Lecture de Paul Celan." Lignes. (1): 147–161.

Buhr, G. (1988). "Von der radikalen In-Frage-Stellung der Kunst in Celans Rede 'Der Meridian.'" Celan-Jahrbuch (2): 169–208.

Gadamer, H.-G. (1985). *Philosophical Apprenticeships*. Translated by Robert R. Sullivan. Cambridge, Mass., The MIT Press.

Glenn, J. (1973). *Paul Celan*. New York, Twayne Publishers, Inc.

Hamacher, W. (1985). "The Second of Inversion: Movements of a Figure through Celan's Poetry." Yale French Studies. (69): 276–314. Reprinted in Fioretos, Aris, ed. Word Traces. (1994). Baltimore. The Johns Hopkins University Press.

Lyon, J. K. (1974). "Paul Celan's Language of Stone: The Geology of the Poetic Landscape." CG. (3/4): 298–317.

Lyon, J. K. (1987). "Die (Patho-)Physiologie des Ichs in der Lyrik Paul Celans." Zeitschrift für Deutsche Philologie.106(4)

Mayer, H. (1970). "Errinnerung an Paul Celan." Merkur. (24): 1160.

Petuchowski, E. (1978). "Bilingual and Multilingual *Wortspiele* in the Poetry of Paul Celan." DVjs.: 635–651.

Podewils, C. (1971). "Namen. Ein Vermächtnis Paul Celans." ensemble. (2): 67–70.

Pöggeler, O. (1986). *Spur des Wortes*. München, Verlag Larl Alber.

Scholem, G. (1960). *Zur Kabbala und ihrer Symbolik.* Zürich, Rhein-Verlag.

Steiner, G. (1976). *A terrible exactness.* The Times Literary Supplement. 709–710.

Wienold, G. (1968). "Paul Celans Hölderlin-Widerruf." Poetica. (2): 216–28.

I^1

Du DARFST[2] mich getrost
mit Schnee[3] bewirten:
sooft ich Schulter an Schulter
mit dem Maulbeerbaum schritt durch den Sommer,
schrie sein jüngstes
Blatt.

You may confidently
regale me with snow:
as often as I strode through summer
shoulder to shoulder with the mulberry tree,
its youngest leaf
shrieked.

see 94

how

VON UNGETRÄUMTEM[4] geätzt,
wirft das schlaflos durchwanderte Brotland
den Lebensberg auf.

Aus seiner Krume
knetest du neu unsre Namen,
die ich, ein deinem
gleichendes
Aug an jedem der Finger,
abtaste nach
einer Stelle, durch die ich
mich zu dir heranwachen kann,
die helle
Hungerkerze im Mund.

BY THE UNDREAMT etched,
the sleeplessly wandered-through breadland
casts up the life mountain.

From its crumb
you knead anew our names,
which I, an eye
similar
to yours on each finger,
probe for
a place, through which I
can wake myself toward you,
the bright
hungercandle in mouth.

IN DIE RILLEN
der Himmelssäure im Türspalt
preßt du das Wort,
dem ich entrollte,
als ich mit bebenden Fäusten
das Dach über uns
abtrug, Schiefer um Schiefer,
Silbe um Silbe, dem Kupfer-
schimmer der Bettel-
schale dort oben
zulieb.

INTO THE FURROWS
of heavenacid in the doorcrack
you press the word
from which I rolled,
when I with trembling fists
the roof over us
dismantled, slate for slate,
syllable for syllable, for the copper-
glimmer of the begging-
cup's sake up
there.

IN DEN FLÜSSEN nördlich der Zukunft
werf ich das Netz aus, das du
zögernd beschwerst
mit von Steinen geschriebenen
Schatten.

IN THE RIVERS north of the future
I cast the net, which you
hesitantly weight
with shadows stones
wrote.

VOR DEIN SPÄTES GESICHT
allein-
gängerisch zwischen
auch mich verwandelnden Nächten,
kam etwas zu stehn,
das schon einmal bei uns war, un-
berührt von Gedanken.

BEFORE YOUR LATE FACE,
a loner
wandering between
nights that change me too,
something came to stand,
which was with us once already, un-
touched by thoughts.

DIE SCHWERMUTSSCHNELLEN HINDURCH,
am blanken
Wundenspiegel vorbei:
da werden die vierzig
entrindeten Lebensbäume geflößt.

Einzige Gegen-
schwimmerin, du
zählst sie, berührst sie
alle.

Down melancholy's rapids
past the blank
woundmirror:
there the forty
stripped lifetrees are rafted.

Single counter-
swimmer, you
count them, touch them
all.

DIE ZAHLEN, im Bund
mit der Bilder Verhängnis
und Gegen-
verhängnis.

Der drübergestülpte
Schädel, an dessen
schlafloser Schläfe ein irr-
lichternder Hammer
all das im Welttakt
besingt.

THE NUMBERS, in league
with the images' doom
and counter-
doom.

The clapped-on
skull, at whose
sleepless temple a will-
of-the-wisping hammer
celebrates all that in
worldbeat.

WEGE IM SCHATTEN-GEBRÄCH[5]
deiner Hand.

Aus der Vier-Finger-Furche[6]
wühl ich mir den
versteinerten Segen.

PATHS IN THE SHADOW-BREAK
of your hand.

From the four-finger-furrow
I root up the
petrified blessing.

WEISSGRAU aus-
geschachteten steilen
Gefühls.

Landeinwärts, hierher-
verwehter Strandhafer bläst
Sandmuster über
den Rauch von Brunnengesängen.

Ein Ohr, abgetrennt, lauscht.

Ein Aug, in Streifen geschnitten,
wird all dem gerecht.

WHITEGRAY of
shafted, steep
feeling.

Landinwards, hither
drifted sea-oats blow
sand patterns over
the smoke of wellchants.

An ear, severed, listens.

An eye, cut in strips,
does justice to all this.

MIT ERDWÄRTS GESUNGENEN MASTEN
fahren die Himmelwracks.

In dieses Holzlied
beißt du dich fest mit den Zähnen.

Du bist der liedfeste
Wimpel.

WITH MASTS SUNG EARTHWARDS
the sky-wrecks drive.

Onto this woodsong
you hold fast with your teeth.

You are the songfast
pennant.

SCHLÄFENZANGE,
von deinem Jochbein beäugt.
Ihr Silberglanz da,
wo sie sich festbiß:
du und der Rest deines Schlafs—
bald
habt ihr Geburtstag.

TEMPLECLAMPS,
eyed by your jugalbone.
Its silverglare there
where they gripped:
you and the rest of your sleep—
soon
will be your birthday.

BEIM HAGELKORN, im
brandigen Mais-
kolben, daheim,
den späten, den harten
Novembersternen gehorsam:

in den Herzfaden die
Gespräche der Würmer geknüpft—:

eine Sehne, von der
deine Pfeilschrift schwirrt,
Schütze.

NEXT TO THE HAILSTONE, in
the mildewed corn-
cob, home,
to the late, the hard
November stars obedient:

in the heartthread, the
knit of worm-talk—:

a bowstring, from which
your arrowscript whirrs,
archer.

STEHEN, im Schatten
des Wundenmals in der Luft.

Für-niemand-und-nichts-Stehn.
Unerkannt,
für dich
allein.

Mit allem, was darin Raum hat,
auch ohne
Sprache.

To STAND, in the shadow
of the stigma in the air.

Standing-for-no-one-and-nothing.
Unrecognized,
for you
alone.

With all that has room in it,
even without
language.

DEIN VOM WACHEN stößiger Traum[7].
Mit der zwölfmal schrauben-
förmig in sein
Horn[8] gekerbten
Wortspur.

Der letzte Stoß, den er führt.

Die in der senk-
rechten, schmalen
Tagschlucht nach oben
stakende Fähre:

sie setzt
Wundgelesenes über.

YOUR DREAM, butting from the watch.
With the wordspoor carved
twelve times
helically into its
horn.   — false dream

The last butt it delivers.

In the ver-
tical narrow
daygorge, the upward
poling ferry:

It carries
sore readings over.

Marginalia:
2 gates
dream
horn
I'm
Aeneas
Energy
Styx
Word

MIT DEN VERFOLGTEN in spätem, un-
verschwiegenem,
strahlendem
Bund.

Das Morgen-Lot,[9] übergoldet,
heftet sich dir an die mit-
schwörende, mit-
schürfende, mit-
schreibende
Ferse.

WITH THE PERSECUTED in late, un-
silenced,
radiating
league.

The morning-plumb, gilded,
hafts itself to your co-
swearing, co-
scratching, co-
writing
heel.

FADENSONNEN[10]
über der grauschwarzen Ödnis.
Ein baum-
hoher Gedanke
greift sich den Lichtton:[11] es sind
noch Lieder zu singen jenseits
der Menschen.

THREADSUNS
above the grayblack wastes.
A tree-
high thought
grasps the light-tone: there are
still songs to sing beyond
mankind.

Im Schlangenwagen [12], an
der weißen Zypresse vorbei,
durch die Flut
fuhren sie dich.

Doch in dir, von
Geburt,
schäumte die andre Quelle,
am schwarzen
Strahl Gedächtnis
klommst du zutag.

IN THE SERPENTCOACH, past
the white cypress,
through the flood
they drove you.

But in you, from
birth,
foamed the other spring,
up the black
ray memory
you climbed to the day.

HARNISCHSTRIEMEN,[13] Faltenachsen,
Durchstich-
punkte:[14]
dein Gelände.

An beiden Polen[15]
der Kluftrose,[16] lesbar:
dein geächtetes Wort.
Nordwahr. Südhell.

Slickensides, fold-axes,
rechanneling-
points:
your terrain.

On both poles
of the cleftrose, legible:
your outlawed word.
Northtrue. Southbright.

WORTAUFSCHÜTTUNG, vulkanisch,
meerüberrauscht.

Oben
der flutende Mob
der Gegengeschöpfe: er
flaggte—Abbild und Nachbild
kreuzen eitel zeithin.

Bis du den Wortmond hinaus-
schleuderst, von dem her
das Wunder Ebbe geschieht
und der herz-
förmige Krater
nackt für die Anfänge zeugt,
die Königs-
geburten.

WORDACCRETION, volcanic,
drowned out by searoar.

Above,
the flooding mob
of the contra-creatures: it
flew a flag—portrait and replica
cruise vainly timeward.

Till you hurl forth the word-
moon, out of which
the wonder ebb occurs
and the heart-
shaped crater
testifies naked for the beginnings,
the kings-
births.

(ICH KENNE DICH, du bist die tief Gebeugte,
ich, der Durchbohrte, bin dir untertan.
Wo flammt ein Wort, das für uns beide zeugte?
Du—ganz, ganz wirklich. Ich—ganz Wahn.)[17]

(I KNOW YOU, you are the deeply bowed,
I, the transpierced, am subject to you.
Where flames a word, would testify for us both?
You—all, all real. I—all delusion.)

WEGGEBEIZT vom
Strahlenwind deiner Sprache
das bunte Gerede des An-
erlebten—das hundert-
züngige Mein-[18]
gedicht, das Genicht.

Aus-
gewirbelt,
frei
der Weg durch den menschen-
gestaltigen Schnee,
den Büßerschnee, zu
den gastlichen
Gletscherstuben und -tischen.

Tief
in der Zeitenschrunde,
beim
Wabeneis
wartet, ein Atemkristall,
dein unumstößliches
Zeugnis.

ERODED by
the beamwind of your speech
the gaudy chatter of the pseudo-
experienced—my hundred-
tongued perjury-
poem, the noem.

Hollow-
whirled,
free
the path through the men-
shaped snow,
the penitent's snow, to
the hospitable
glacier-parlors and -tables.

Deep
in the timecrevasse,
in the
honeycomb-ice,
waits a breathcrystal,
your unalterable
testimony.

II

VOM GROSSEN
Augen-
losen
aus deinen Augen geschöpft:

der sechs-
kantige, absageweiße
Findling.[19]

Eine Blindenhand, sternhart auch sie
vom Namen-Durchwandern,
ruht auf ihm, so
lang wie auf dir,
Esther.[20]

BY THE GREAT
Eye-
less
scooped from your eyes:

the six-
edged, denialwhite
erratic.

A blind man's hand, it also starhard
from name-wandering,
rests on him, as
long as on you,
Esther.

SINGBARER REST—der Umriß
dessen, der durch
die Sichelschrift lautlos hindurchbrach,
abseits, am Schneeort.

Quirlend
unter Kometen-
brauen
die Blickmasse, auf
die der verfinsterte winzige
Herztrabant zutreibt
mit dem
draußen erjagten Funken.

—Entmündigte Lippe, melde,
daß etwas geschieht, noch immer,
unweit von dir.

Singable remnant—the outline
of him, who through
the sicklescript broke through unvoiced,
apart, at the snowplace.

Whirling
under comet-
brows,
the gaze's bulk, towards
which the eclipsed, tiny
heart-satellite drifts
with the
spark caught outside.

—Disenfranchised lip, announce,
that something happens, still,
not far from you.

FLUTENDER, groß-
zelliger Schlafbau.

Jede
Zwischenwand von
Graugeschwadern befahren.

Es scheren die Buchstaben aus,
die letzten
traumdichten Kähne—
jeder mit einem
Teil des noch
zu versenkenden Zeichens
im
geierkralligen Schlepptau.

FLOWING, big-
celled sleepingden.

Each
partition travelled
by graysquadrons.

The letters are breaking formation,
the last
dreamproof skiffs—
each with
part of the still
to be sunken sign
in
the towrope's vulturegrip.

ZWANZIG FÜR IMMER
verflüchtigte Schlüsselburg-Blumen[21]
in deiner schwimmenden linken
Faust.

In die Fisch-
schuppe geätzt:
die Linien der Hand,
der sie entwuchsen.

Himmels- und Erd-
säure flossen zusammen.
Die Zeit-
rechnung ging auf, ohne Rest. Es kreuzen
—dir, schnelle Schwermut, zulieb—
Schuppe und Faust.

TWENTY FOREVER
evaporated Keytower-flowers
in your swimming left
fist.

Into the fish-
scale etched:
the lines of the hand
which they outgrew.

Heaven- and earth-
acid flowed together.
The time-
reckoning worked out, without remainder. Cruising:
—for your, quick melancholy, sake—
scale and fist.

KEINE SANDKUNST MEHR, kein Sandbuch, keine Meister.

Nichts erwürfelt. Wieviel
Stumme?
Siebenzehn.

Deine Frage—deine Antwort.
Dein Gesang, was weiß er?

Tiefimschnee,

       Iefimnee,

             I—i—e.

No SANDART ANYMORE, no sandbook, no masters.

Nothing in the dice. How
many mutes?
Seventen.

Your question—your answer.
Your chant, what does it know?

Deepinsnow,
            Eepinno,
                    I—i—o.

HELLIGKEITSHUNGER—mit ihm
ging ich die Brot-
stufe hinauf,
unter die Blinden-
glocke:

sie, die wasser-
klare,
stülpt sich über
die mitgestiegene, mit-
verstiegene Freiheit, an der
einer der Himmel sich sattfraß,
den ich sich wölben ließ über
der wortdurchschwommenen
Bildbahn, Blutbahn.

BRIGHTNESSHUNGER—with it
I walked up the bread-
step, under
the blindness-
bell:

it, water-
clear,
claps itself over
the freedom that climbed with
me, that with me climbed
too high, on which
one of the heavens gorged itself,
that I let vault above
the worddrenched
image orbit, blood orbit.

ALS UNS DAS WEISSE ANFIEL, nachts;
als aus dem Spendekrug mehr
kam als Wasser;
als das geschundene Knie
der Opferglocke den Wink gab:
Flieg!—

Da
war ich
noch ganz.

WHEN WHITENESS ASSAILED US, AT NIGHT;
when from the libation-ewer more
than water came;
when the skinned knee
gave the sacrificebell the nod:
Fly!—

Then
I still
was whole.

HOHLES LEBENSGEHÖFT. Im Windfang
die leer-
geblasene Lunge
blüht. Eine Handvoll
Schlafkorn
weht aus dem wahr-
gestammelten Mund
hinaus zu den Schnee-
gesprächen.

HOLLOW LIFEHOMESTEAD. In the windtrap
the lung
blown empty
flowers. A handful
sleepcorn
drifts from the mouth
stammered true
out towards the snow-
conversations.

ÜBER DREI im meer-
trunkenen Schlaf
mit Braunalgenblut
bezifferte Brust-
warzensteine

stülp deinen sich
von der letzten
Regenschnur los-
reißenden Himmel.

Und laß
deine mit dir hierher-
gerittene Süßwassermuschel

all das hinunter-
schlürfen, bevor
du sie ans Ohr
eines Uhrschattens hältst,
abends.

OVER THREE in sea-
drunken sleep
with brownalgae-blood
ciphered breast-
nipplestones

clap your
from the last
raincord breaking
loose sky.

And let
your freshwatermussel that rode
with you to this place

lap all that
up, before
you hold her to the ear
of a clock's shadow,
evenings.

AM WEISSEN GEBETRIEMEN[22]—der
Herr dieser Stunde
war
ein Wintergeschöpf, ihm
zulieb
geschah, was geschah—
biß sich mein kletternder Mund fest, noch einmal,
als er dich suchte, Rauchspur
du, droben,
in Frauengestalt,
du auf der Reise zu meinen
Feuergedanken im Schwarzkies
jenseits der Spaltworte, durch
die ich dich gehn sah, hoch-
beinig und
den schwerlippigen eignen
Kopf
auf dem von meinen
tödlich genauen
Händen
lebendigen Körper.

ON THE WHITE PHILACTERY—the
Lord of this hour
was
a wintercreature, for his
sake
happened what happened—
my climbing mouth bit in, once more,
when it looked for you, smoketrace
you, up there,
in woman's shape,
you on the journey to my
firethoughts in the blackgravel
beyond the cleftwords, through
which I saw you walk, high-
legged and
the heavylipped own
head
on the by my
deadly accurate
hands
living body.

Sag deinen dich
bis in die Schluchten hinein-
begleitenden Fingern, wie
ich dich kannte, wie weit
ich dich ins Tiefe stieß, wo
dich mein bitterster Traum
herzher beschlief, im Bett
meines unablösbaren Namens.

Tell your fingers
accompanying you far in-
side the crevasses, how
I knew you, how far
I pushed you into the deep,
where my most bitter dream
slept with you heart-fro, in the bed
of my inextinguishable name.

ERBLINDE schon heut:
auch die Ewigkeit steht voller Augen—
darin
ertrinkt, was den Bildern hinweghalf
über den Weg, den sie kamen,
darin
erlischt, was auch dich aus der Sprache
fortnahm mit einer Geste,
die du geschehn ließt wie
den Tanz zweier Worte aus lauter
Herbst und Seide und Nichts.

Go BLIND today already:
eternity too is full of eyes—
wherein
drowns, what helped the images
over the path they came,
wherein
expires, what took you too out of
language with a gesture
that you let happen like
the dance of two words of just
autumn and silk and nothingness.

ENGHOLZTAG unter
netznervigem Himmelblatt. Durch
großzellige Leerstunden klettert, im Regen,
der schwarzblaue, der
Gedankenkäfer.

Tierblütige[23] Worte
drängen sich vor seine Fühler.

NARROWWOOD DAY under
netnerved skyleaf. Through
bigcelled idlehours clambers, in rain,
the blackblue, the
thoughtbeetle.

Animal-bloodsoming words
crowd before its feelers.

HEUTE:
Nächtliches, wieder, feuergepeitscht.
Glosender
Nacktpflanzenreigen.

(Gestern:
über den rudernden Namen
schwebte die Treue;
Kreide ging schreibend umher;
offen lag es und grüßte:
das wassergewordene Buch.)

Den Eulenkiesel erlost—
vom Schlafsims
blickt er herunter
aufs Fünfaug, dem du verfielst.

Sonst?
Halb- und Viertel-
verbündete auf
der Geschlagenen-Seite. Reichtümer an
verloren-vergällter
Sprache.

TODAY:
nightthings, again, fire whipped.
Glowing
naked-plants-dance.

(Yesterday:
above the rowing names
floated faithfulness;
chalk went around writing;
open it laid and greeted:
the turned-to-water book.)

The owlpebble raffled—
from the sleepcornice
he looks down
upon the five-eye, to whom you devolved.

Otherwise?
Half- and quarter-
allies on
the side of the beaten. Riches of
lost-soured
language.

Wenn sie den letzten
Schatten pfählen,
brennst du die schwörende Hand frei.

When they impale
the last shadow,
you burn the vowing hand free.

MITTAGS, bei
Sekundengeflirr,
im Rundgräberschatten, in meinen
gekammerten Schmerz
—mit dir, Herbei-
geschwiegene, lebt ich
zwei Tage in Rom
von Ocker und Rot—
kommst du, ich liege schon da,
hell durch die Türen geglitten, waagrecht—:

es werden die Arme sichtbar, die dich umschlingen, nur sie.
    [Soviel

Geheimnis
bot ich noch auf, trotz allem.

MIDDAY, with
seconds' flurry,
in the roundgraveshadow, into my
chambered pain
—with you, hither-
silenced, I lived
two days in Rome
on ocher and red—
you come, I already lie there,
gliding light through the doors, horizontal—:

the arms holding you become visible, only they. That much

secrecy
I still summoned, in spite of all.

UNTER DIE HAUT meiner Hände genäht:
dein mit Händen
getrösteter Name.

Wenn ich den Klumpen Luft
knete, unsere Nahrung,
säuert ihn der
Buchstabenschimmer aus
der wahnwitzig-offenen
Pore.

Sown under the skin of my hands:
your name comforted
by hands:

When I knead the lump
of air, our nourishment,
it is leavened by the
letters' shimmer from
the lunatic-open
pore.

DAS STUNDENGLAS, tief
im Päonienschatten vergraben:

Wenn das Denken die Pfingst-
schneise herabkommt, endlich,
fällt ihm das Reich zu,
wo du versandend verhoffst.[24]

THE HOURGLASS, deep
in peonyshadow, buried:

When Thinking comes down
the Pentecost-lane, finally,
it inherits that empire,
where you, bogged down, scent.

HAFEN

Wundgeheilt: wo-,
wenn du wie ich wärst, kreuz-
und quergeträumt von
Schnapsflaschenhälsen am
Hurentisch

—würfel
mein Glück zurecht, Meerhaar,
schaufel die Welle zuhauf, die mich trägt, Schwarzfluch,
brich dir den Weg
durch den heißesten Schoß,
Eiskummerfeder—,

wo-
hin
kämst du nicht mit mir zu liegen, auch
auf die Bänke
bei Mutter Clausen, ja sie
weiß, wie oft ich dir bis
in die Kehle hinaufsang, heidideldu,
wie die heidelbeerblaue
Erle der Heimat mit all ihrem Laub,
heidudeldi,
du, wie die

HARBOR

Sorehealed: where-,
when you were like me, criss-
and crossdreamt by
schnappsbottlenecks at the
whore table

—cast
my happiness aright, Seahair,
heap up the wave, that carries me, Blackcurse,
break your way
through the hottest womb,
Icesorrowpen—,

where-
to
didn't you come to lie with me, even
on the benches
at Mother Clausen's, yes, she
knows, how often I sang all
the way up into your throat, hey-diddle-doo,
like the bilberryblue
alder of homeland with all its leaves,
hey-doodle-dee,
you, like the

Astralflöte von
jenseits des Weltgrats—auch da
schwammen wir, Nacktnackte, schwammen,
den Abgrundvers auf
brandroter Stirn—unverglüht grub
sich das tief-
innen flutende Gold
seine Wege nach oben—,

                    hier,
mit bewimperten Segeln,
fuhr auch Erinnrung vorbei, langsam
sprangen die Brände hinüber, ab-
getrennt, du,
abgetrennt auf
den beiden blau-
schwarzen Gedächtnis-
schuten,
doch angetrieben auch jetzt
vom Tausend-
arm, mit dem ich dich hielt,
kreuzen, an Sternwurf-Kaschemmen vorbei,
unsre immer noch trunknen, trinkenden,
nebenweltlichen Münder—ich nenne nur sie—,

bis drüben am zeitgrünen Uhrturm
die Netz-, die Ziffernhaut lautlos
sich ablöst—ein Wahndock,

astralflute from
beyond the worldridge—there too
we swam, nakednudes, swam,
the abyssverse on
the fire red forehead—unconsumed by
fire the deep-
inside flooding gold
dug its paths upwards—,

                    here,
with eyelashed sails,
remembrance too drove past, slowly
the conflagration jumped over, cut-
off, you,
cut off on
the two blue-
black memory-
barges,
but driven on now also
by the thousand-
arm, with which I held you,
they cruise, past starthrow-dives,
our still drunk, still drinking
byworldly mouths—I name only them—

till over there at the timegreen clocktower
the net-, the numberskin soundlessly
peels off—a delusion-dock,

schwimmend, davor
abweltweiß die
Buchstaben der
Großkräne einen
Unnamen schreiben, an dem
klettert sie hoch, zum Todessprung, die
Laufkatze[25] Leben,
den
baggern die sinn-
gierigen Sätze nach Mitternacht aus,
nach ihm
wirft die neptunische Sünde ihr korn-
schnapsfarbenes Schleppseil,
zwischen
zwölf-
tonigen Liebeslautbojen
—Ziehbrunnenwinde damals, mit dir
singt es im nicht mehr
binnenländischen Chor—
kommen die Leuchtfeuerschiffe getanzt,
weither, aus Odessa,

die Tieflademarke,
die mit uns sinkt, unsrer Last treu,
eulenspiegelt[26] das alles
hinunter, hinauf und—warum nicht? *wundgeheilt, wo—,*

wenn—

herbei und vorbei und herbei.

swimming, before it,
off-world-white the
letters of the
great cranes write
an unname, which
she clambers up, to the deathjump, the
cat, the trolley, life, which
the sense-
greedy sentences dredge up, after
midnight,
at which
neptunic sin throws its corn-
schnapps-colored towrope,
between
twelve-
toned lovesoundbuoys
—draw-well-winch back then, with you
it sings in the no longer
inland choir—
the beaconlightships come dancing,
from afar, from Odessa,

the loadline,
which sinks with us, true to our burden,
Owlglasses all that
downwards, upwards, and why not? *sorehealed, where-,*

when-

hither and past and hither.

III

SCHWARZ,
wie die Erinnerungswunde,
wühlen die Augen nach dir
in dem von Herzzähnen hell-
gebissenen Kronland,
das unser Bett bleibt:

durch diesen Schacht mußt du kommen—
du kommst.

Im Samen-
sinn
sternt dich das Meer aus, zuinnerst, für immer.

Das Namengeben hat ein Ende,
über dich werf ich mein Schicksal.

BLACK,
like the memory-wound,
the eyes dig toward you,
in the by heartteeth light-
bitten crownland,
that remains our bed:

through this shaft you have to come—
you come.

In seed-
sense
the sea stars you out, innermost, forever.

The namegiving has an end,
over you I cast my lot.

HAMMERKÖPFIGES, im
Zeltgang,
neben uns her, der doppelten,
langsam strömenden Rotspur.

Silbriges:
Hufsprüche, Schlaflied-
gewieher—Traum-
hürde und -wehr—: niemand
soll weiter, nichts.

Dich unter mir, kentaurisch
gebäumt,
münd ich in unsern hinüber-
rauschenden Schatten.

HAMMERHEADEDNESS, at
palfrey pace,
alongside us, of the double
slowly streaming redtrack.

Silvery:
Hoofsayings, lullaby-
neighing—dream-
hurdle and -weir—: no one
shall go further, nothing.

You under me, centaurishly
rearing,
I empty into our across-
roaring shadow.

LANDSCHAFT mit Urnenwesen.
Gespräche
von Rauchmund zu Rauchmund.

Sie essen:
die Tollhäusler-Trüffel, ein Stück
unvergrabner Poesie,
fand Zunge und Zahn.

Eine Träne rollt in ihr Auge zurück.

Die linke, verwaiste
Hälfte der Pilger-
muschel—sie schenkten sie dir,
dann banden sie dich—
leuchtet lauschend den Raum aus:

das Klinkerspiel gegen den Tod
kann beginnen.

Landscape with urnbeings.
Conversations
from smokemouth to smokemouth.

They eat:
the bedlamite's truffle, a piece
unburied poetry,
found tongue and tooth.

A tear rolls back into its eye.

The left, orphaned
half of the pilgrim-
mussel—they gave it to you,
then they bound you—
listening it illuminates the space:

the clinkergame against death
can begin.

DIE GAUKLERTROMMEL,
von meinem Herzgroschen laut.

Die Sprossen der Leiter, über
die Odysseus, mein Affe, nach Ithaka klettert,
rue de Longchamp, eine Stunde
nach dem verschütteten Wein:

tu das zum Bild,
das uns heimwürfelt in
den Becher, in dem ich bei dir lieg,
unausspielbar.

THE JUGGLERDRUM,
from my heartpenny loud.

The rungs of the ladder, up
which Ulysses, my monkey, clambers toward Ithaca,
rue de Longchamp, one hour
after the spilled wine:

add that to the image,
which casts us home into
the dicecup, where I lie by you,
unplayable.

WENN DU IM BETT
aus verschollenem Fahnentuch liegst,
bei blauschwarzen Silben, im Schneewimperschatten,
kommt, durch Gedanken-
güsse,
der Kranich geschwommen, stählern—
du öffnest dich ihm.

Sein Schnabel tickt dir die Stunde
in jeden Mund—in jeder
glöcknert, mit glutrotem Strang, ein Schweige-
Jahrtausend,
Unfrist und Frist
münzen einander zutode,
die Taler, die Groschen
regnen dir hart durch die Poren,
in
Sekundengestalt
fliegst du hin und verrammelst
die Türen Gestern und Morgen,—phosphorn,
wie Ewigkeitszähne,
knospt deine eine, knospt auch die
andere Brust,
den Griffen entgegen, unter

WHEN YOU LIE
in the bed of missing bunting,
by blueblack syllables, in the
shadow of snowlashes,
through thought-showers the steely
crane comes swimming—
you open yourself to him.

His bill ticks you the hour
into each mouth—in each
chimes, with bloodred bell-rope, a silence-
millennium,
the hour and the reprieve
coin each other to death,
the taler, the groschen
rain hard through your pores
in
the shape of a second
you fly there and barricade
the doors Yesterday and Tomorrow,—phosphorous
like eternityteeth,
buds your one, then your other
breast,
toward the grips, under

den Stößen—: so dicht,
so tief
gestreut
ist der sternige
Kranich-
Same.

the strokes——: so tightly,
so deeply
sown
is the starry
crane-
seed.

HINTERM KOHLEGEZINKTEN Schlaf
—man kennt unsre Kate—,
wo uns der Traumkamm schwoll, feurig, trotz allem,
und ich die Goldnägel trieb in unser
nebenher sargschön
schwimmendes Morgen,

da schnellten die Ruten königlich vor unserm Aug,
Wasser kam, Wasser,
bissig
gruben sich Kähne voran durch die Großsekunde Gedächtnis,
es trieb das Getier mit den Schlamm-Mäulern um uns
—so viel
fing noch kein Himmel—,
was warst du, Zerrissene, doch
wieder für eine Reuse!—, trieb das Getier, das Getier,

Salzhorizonte
bauten an unsern Blicken, es wuchs ein Gebirg
weit hinaus in die Schlucht,
in der meine Welt die deine
aufbot, für immer.

Behind coalmarked sleep
—our cottage is known—
where our dreamcrest swelled, fiery, despite all,
and I the goldnails drove into our
coffin-beautiful morning
swimming alongside,

there the rods dipped royally before our eye,
water came, water,
savagely
the skiffs bit through the grand-second memory,
the mud-muzzled beasts drifted around us
—that much
no heaven caught yet—,
what a weir, torn one,
you were, once again!—, the beasts, the beasts, adrift,

salthorizons
were building on our glances, a mountain grew
far outward into the ravine,
where my world summoned
yours, forever.

IN PRAG[27]

Der halbe Tod,[28]
großgesäugt mit unserm Leben,
lag aschenbildwahr um uns her—

auch wir
tranken noch immer, seelenverkreuzt, zwei Degen,
an Himmelssteine genäht, wortblutgeboren
im Nachtbett,

größer und größer
wuchsen wir durcheinander, es gab
keinen Namen mehr für
das, was uns trieb (einer der Wieviel-
unddreißig[29]
war mein lebendiger Schatten,
der die Wahnstiege hochklomm zu dir?),

ein Turm,
baute der Halbe sich ins Wohin,
ein Hradschin
aus lauter Goldmacher-Nein,[30]

IN PRAGUE

Half-death,
suckled on our life,
lay ash-image-true around us—

we too
kept on drinking, soul-crossed, two swords,
stitched to heavenstones, born of wordblood,
in the nightbed,

larger and larger
we grew, intergrafted, there was
no name left for
what urged us on (one of thirty-
-and-how-many
was my living shadow,
who climbed up the delusion-stairs to you?)

a tower,
the half-one built into the Whither,
a Hradčany
all of goldmaker's No,

Knochen-Hebräisch,
zu Sperma zermahlen,[31]
rann durch die Sanduhr,
die wir durchschwammen, zwei Träume jetzt, läutend
wider die Zeit, auf den Plätzen.

bone-Hebrew,
ground to sperm,
ran through the hourglass,
through which we swam, two dreams now, tolling
against time, on the squares.

VON DER ORCHIS HER—
geh, zähl
die Schatten der Schritte zusammen bis zu ihr
hinterm Fünfgebirg Kindheit—,
von ihr her, der
ich das Halbwort abgewinn für die Zwölfnacht,
kommt meine Hand dich zu greifen
für immer.

Ein kleines Verhägnis, so groß
wie der Herzpunkt, den ich
hinter dein meinen Namen
stammelndes Aug setz,
ist mir behilflich.

       Du kommst auch,
wie über Wiesen,
und bringst das Bild einer Kaimauer mit,
da würfelten, als
unsre Schlüssel, tief im Verwehrten,
sich kreuzten in Wappengestalt,
Fremde mit dem, was
wir beide noch immer besitzen
an Sprache,
an Schicksal.

Starting from the Orchis—
go, count
the shadows of the steps up to it
behind the five-mountain childhood—,
from it, I win
the half-word for the twelve-night, from it
comes my hand to grab you
forever.

A little doom, as big
as the heartdot I set
behind your my name
stammering eye,
is helpful to me.

                You also come,
as if over meadows,
and bring along the image of a quaywall,
there—when
our keys, deep in the refused,
crossed each other heraldically—
strangers play dice with what
we both still own
of language,
of destiny.

HALBZERFRESSENER, masken-
gesichtiger Kragstein,
tief
in der Augenschlitz-Krypta:

Hinein, hinauf
ins Schädelinnre,
wo du den Himmel umbrichst, wieder und wieder,
in Furche und Windung
pflanzt er sein Bild,
das sich entwächst, entwächst.

HALF-GNAWED, mask-
miened corbel stone,
deep
in the eyeslit-crypt:

Inward, upward
into skull's inside,
where you break up heaven, again and again,
into furrow and convolution
he plants his image,
which outgrows and outgrows itself.

AUS FÄUSTEN, weiß
von der aus der Wortwand
freigehämmerten Wahrheit,
erblüht dir ein neues Gehirn.

Schön, durch nichts zu verschleiern,
wirft es sie, die
Gedankenschatten.
Darin, unverrückbar,
falten sich, heut noch,
zwölf Berge, zwölf Stirnen.

Die auch von dir her stern-
äugige Streunerin Schwermut
erfährts.[32]

FROM FISTS, white
from the truth hammered
free of the wordwall,
a new brain blooms for you.

Beautiful, to be veiled by nothing,
it casts them, the
thoughtshadows.
Therein, immovable,
fold up, even today,
twelve mountains, twelve foreheads.

The from you also star-
eyed loafer Melancholy
hears of it.

SCHWIRRHÖLZER [33] fahren ins Licht, die Wahrheit
gibt Nachricht.

Drüben die Ufer-
böschung schwillt uns entgegen,
ein dunkler
Tausendglanz—die
auferstandenen Häuser!—
singt.

Ein Eisdorn—auch wir
hatten gerufen—
versammelt die Klänge.

BULLROARERS whizz into the light, truth
sends word.

Yonder, the shore's
slope swells toward us,
a dark
thousand-brightness—the
ressurrected houses!—
sings.

An icethorn—we too
had called—
gathers the tones.

ABENDS, in
Hamburg, ein
unendlicher Schuhriemen—an
ihm
kauen die Geister—
bindet zwei blutige Zehen zusammen
zum Wegschwur.

EVENING, in
Hamburg, an
endless shoestring—at
which
the ghosts gnaw—
binds two bloody toes together
for the road's oath.

BEI DEN ZUSAMMENGETRETENEN
Zeichen, im
worthäutigen Ölzelt, am Ausgang
der Zeit,
hellgestöhnt
ohne Laut
—du, Königsluft, ans
Pestkreuz genagelte, jetzt,
blühst du—,
porenäugig,
schmerzgeschuppt, zu
Pferde.

AT THE ASSEMBLED
signs, in the
wordmembraned oiltent, at the outlet
of time,
groaned into brightness
soundlessly
—you, king's air, nailed
to the plaguecross, now
you bloom—,
pore-eyed,
pain-scaly, on
horseback.

DAS AUFWÄRTSSTEHENDE LAND,
rissig,
mit der Flugwurzel, der
Steinatem zuwächst.

Auch hier
stürzen die Meere hinzu, aus der Steilschlucht,
und dein sprach-
pockiger, panischer
Ketzer
kreuzt.

THE UPWARDS-STANDING COUNTRY,
cracked,
with the flightroot, to which
stonebreath accrues.

Here also
the seas rush in, out of the steep ravine,
and your speech-
pocked, panic
heretic
cruises.

DAS UMHERGESTOSSENE
Immer-Licht, lehmgelb,
hinter
Planetenhäuptern.

Erfundene
Blicke, Seh-
narben,
ins Raumschiff gekerbt,
betteln um Erden-
münder.

THE PUSHED-AROUND
ever-light, loam yellow,
behind
planetheads.

Invented
looks, see-
scars,
carved into the spaceship,
beg for earth-
mouths.

ASCHENGLORIE hinter
deinen erschüttert-verknoteten
Händen am Dreiweg.

Pontisches Einstmals: hier,
ein Tropfen,
auf
dem ertrunkenen Ruderblatt,
tief
im versteinerten Schwur,
rauscht es auf.

(Auf dem senkrechten
Atemseil, damals,
höher als oben,
zwischen zwei Schmerzknoten, während
der blanke
Tatarenmond zu uns heraufklomm,
grub ich mich in dich und in dich.)

Aschen-
glorie hinter
euch Dreiweg-
Händen.

ASHGLORY behind
your shaken-knotted
hands at the threeway.

Pontic erstwhile: here,
a drop,
on
the drowned rudder blade,
deep
in the petrified oath,
it roars up.

(On the vertical
breathrope, in those days,
higher than above,
between two painknots, while
the glossy
Tatarmoon climbed up to us,
I dug myself into you and into you.)

Ash-
glory behind
you threeway
hands.

Das vor euch, vom Osten her, Hin-
gewürfelte, furchtbar.

Niemand
zeugt für den
Zeugen.

The cast-in-front-of-you, from
the East, terrible.

Nobody
bears witness for the
witness.

IV

DAS GESCHRIEBENE höhlt sich, das
Gesprochene, meergrün,
brennt in den Buchten,

in den
verflüssigten Namen
schnellen die Tümmler,

im geewigten Nirgends, hier,
im Gedächtnis der über-
lauten Glocken in—wo nur?,

wer
in diesem
Schattengeviert
schnaubt, wer
unter ihm
schimmert auf, schimmert auf, schimmert auf?

THE WRITTEN hollows itself, the
spoken, seagreen,
burns in the bays,

in the
liquified names
the dolphins dart,

in the eternalized Nowhere, here,
in the memory of the over-
loud bells in—where only?

who
pants
in this
shadow-quadrat, who
from beneath it
shimmers, shimmers, shimmers?

CELLO-EINSATZ
von hinter dem Schmerz:

die Gewalten, nach Gegen-
himmeln gestaffelt,
wälzen Undeutbares vor
Einflugschneise und Einfahrt,

der
erklommene Abend
steht voller Lungengeäst,

zwei
Brandwolken Atem
graben im Buch,
das der Schläfenlärm aufschlug,

etwas wird wahr,

zwölfmal erglüht
das von Pfeilen getroffene Drüben,

die Schwarz-
blütige[34] trinkt
des Schwarzblütigen Samen,

CELLO-ENTRY
from behind pain:

The powers, escheloned
as the counter-heavens,
roll inexplicables before
approach lane and arrival,

the
scaled evening
stands full of lungbranches,

two
blaze-clouds of breath
dig in the book
which the temple-din opened,

something comes true,

twelve times glows
the arrow-riddled yonder,

she, black-
bloodsommed, drinks
his blackbloodsommed seed,

alles ist weniger, als
es ist,
alles ist mehr.

all is less, than
it is,
all is more.

FRIHED

Im Haus zum gedoppelten Wahn,
wo die Steinboote fliegen
überm
Weißkönigs-Pier, den Geheimnissen zu,
wo das endlich
abgenabelte
Orlog-Wort kreuzt,

bin ich, von Schilfmark Genährte,
in dir, auf
Wildenten-Teichen,

ich singe—

was sing ich?

Der Mantel
des Saboteurs
mit den roten, den weißen
Kreisen um die
Einschuß-
stellen

FRIHED

In the house of the doubled delusion,
where the stoneboats fly
over
Whiteking's pier, toward the secrets,
where with
cord finally cut the
man-of-war-word cruises,

I, reed-pith nourished, am
in you, on
wild ducks' ponds,

I sing—

what do I sing?

The saboteur's
coat
with the red, the white
circles around the
bullet
holes

—durch sie
erblickst du das mit uns fahrende
frei-
sternige Oben—
deckt uns jetzt zu,

der Grünspan-Adel vom Kai,
mit seinen Backstein-Gedanken
rund um die Stirn,
häuft den Geist rings, den Gischt,

schnell
verblühn die Geräusche
diesseits und jenseits der Trauer,

die näher-
segelnde
Eiterzacke der Krone
in eines Schief-
geborenen Aug
dichtet
dänisch.

—through them
you sight the with us driving
free-
starry Above—
covers us now,

the verdigris-nobility from the quay,
with its burned-brick thoughts
round about the forehead,
heaps the spirit round, the spindrift,

quick
the noises wither
this side and that side of mourning,

the crown's
closer-
sailing pusprong
in the eye of one
born crooked
writes poems
in Danish.

DEN VERKIESELTEN SPRUCH in der Faust,
vergißt du, daß du vergißt,

am Handgelenk schießen
blinkend die Satzzeichen an,

durch die zum Kamm
gespaltene Erde
kommen die Pausen geritten,

dort, bei
der Opferstaude,
wo das Gedächtnis entbrennt,
greift euch der Eine
Hauch auf.

THE SILICIFIED SAYING in the fist,
you forget that you forget,

blinking, the punctuation marks
crystallize at the wrist,

through the earth
cleft to the crest
the pauses come riding,

there, by
the sacrifice-bush,
where memory catches fire,
the One Breath
seizes you.

Wo?
In den Lockermassen der Nacht.

Im Gramgeröll und -geschiebe,
im langsamsten Aufruhr,
im Weisheitsschacht Nie.

Wassernadeln
nähn den geborstenen
Schatten zusammen—er kämpft sich
tiefer hinunter,
frei.

WHERE?
In night's friable matter.

In sorrow-débris and -drift,
in slowest uproar,
in the wisdomshaft Never.

Waterneedles
sew the burst
shadow together—it fights its way
deeper down,
free.

KÖNIGSWUT, steinmähnig, vorn.

Und die verrauchten
Gebete—
Hengste, hinzu-
geschmerzt, die
unbezähmbar-gehorsame
Freischar:

psalmhufig, hinsingend über
auf-, auf-, auf-,
geblättertes Bibelgebirg,
auf die klaren, mit-
klirrenden,
mächtigen Meerkeime zu.

KING'S RAGE, stonemaned, up front.

And the prayers,
gone up in smoke—
stallions, pain-
accrued, the
untamable-obedient
irregulars:

psalmhoofed, singing across
open-, open-, open-
leafed Biblemountains,
toward the clear, also
clattering,
mighty seagerms.

SOLVE[35]

Entosteter, zu
Brandscheiten zer-
spaltener Grabbaum:

and den Gift-
pfalzen vorbei, an den Domen,
stromaufwärts, strom-
abwärts geflößt

vom winzig-lodernden, vom
freien
Satzzeichen der
zu den unzähligen zu
nennenden un-
aussprechlichen
Namen aus-
einandergeflohenen, ge-
borgenen
Schrift.

SOLVE

De-easterned tomb-
tree, split into
firebrands:

past the Poison-
Palatinates, past the cathedrals,
upstream, down-
stream, rafted

by the tiny-flaring, by the
free
punctuation mark of the
script salvaged and dis-
solved into the count⁼
less to-be-
named un-
pronounceable
names.

COAGULA

Auch deine
Wunde, Rosa.[36]

Und das Hörnerlicht deiner
rumänischen Büffel
an Sternes Statt überm
Sandbett, im
redenden, rot-
aschengewaltigen
Kolben.

COAGULA

Your wound
too, Rosa.

And the hornslight of your
Rumanian buffaloes
in star's stead above the
sandbed, in the
talking, red-
ember-mighty
alembic.

SCHÄDELDENKEN, stumm, auf der Pfeilspur.

Dein hohes
Lied, in den harten
Februarfunken verbißner,
halbzertrümmerter
Kiefer.

Die eine, noch
zu befahrende Meile
Melancholie.

Von Erreichtem umbuscht jetzt, zielblau,
aufrecht im Kahn,
auch aus dem knirschenden Klippen-
segen entlassen.

SKULLTHINKING, dumb, on the arrowtrace.

Your high
song, into the hard
February-spark clamped,
half-shattered
jaw.

The one, still
to be travelled mile
Melancholy.

Ambushed now by the achieved, aimblue,
upright in the skiff,
also from the gnashing crag-
blessings released.

OSTERQUALM, flutend, mit
der buchstabenähnlichen
Kielspur inmitten.

(Niemals war Himmel.
Doch Meer ist noch, brandrot,
Meer.)

Wir hier, wir,
überfahrtsfroh, vor dem Zelt,
wo du Wüstenbrot bukst
aus mitgewanderter Sprache.

Am äußersten Blickrand: der Tanz
zweier Klingen übers
Herzschattenseil.

Das Netz darunter, geknüpft
aus Gedanken-
enden—in welcher
Tiefe?

Da: der zerbissene
Ewigkeitsgroschen, zu uns
heraufgespien durch die Maschen.

EASTERSMOKE, flooding, with
the letterlike
keeltrack amidst.

(Never was heaven.
But sea still is, fire red,
sea.)

We here, we,
glad for the passage, before the tent,
where you baked desertbread
from wandered-along language.

At the furthest sight-edge: the dance
of two blades across the
heartshadowcord.

The net underneath, knotted
from thought-
ends—at what
depth?

There: the bitten through
eternity-penny, spat
up to us through the meshes.

Drei Sandstimmen, drei
Skorpione:
das Gastvolk, mit uns
im Kahn.

Three sandvoices, three
scorpions:
the guest-people, with us
in the skiff.

KAIMAUER-RAST, rittlings,
im Schatten der
von obenher auf-
gefächerten Trümpfe—

deine
abgegriffenen
Hände, gröber als je,
greifen anderswohin.

Die schöpfende, wieder
und wieder
überschwappende, um-
zugießende Schale voll Galle.

Die leicht
herübergeneigten,
flußaufwärts gesteuerten
Wandergefäße, dicht
an deinem Knieschorf vorbei.

Quader, reit.

Grauglaube neben mir,
trink
mit.

QUAYWALL-REST, astride,
in the shadow of the
trumps fanned open
from above—

your
worn-out
hands, coarser than ever,
reach elsewhere.

The scooping, again
and again
slopping over, to be
spilled, cup full of bile.

The slightly
hither-bent,
upstream-steered
wander-vessels, passing
hard by your kneescab.

Ashlar, ride.

Grayfaith next to me,
drink
up.

ERHÖRT
von den umgebetteten Funken
der Feuerduft um
den Leuchterstachel.

Alle
Bahnen sind frei.

Mehrere Erden
spiel ich dir zu im Erblinden—
die beiden
weißen behälst du, eine
in jeder Hand.

Die Un-
bestatteten, ungezählt, droben,
die Kinder,
sind absprungbereit—

Dir,
Quellnächtige, war
ich nicht ähnlich:
dich, Freudige, wie
du jetzt schwebst,
pfählt der unsichtbare, zweite,
stehende Brand.

210

ANSWERED
by the transferred sparks
the firefragrance around
the pricket.

All
orbits are free.

Several earths
I pass to you while going blind—
the two
white ones you keep, one
in each hand.

The un-
buried, uncounted, up there,
the children,
are ready to jump—

You,
source-nightly, I
did not resemble:
you, joyous, as
you now hover, are
impaled by the invisible, second,
standing firebrand.

SCHAUFÄDEN, SINNFÄDEN, aus
Nachtgalle geknüpft
hinter der Zeit:

wer
ist unsichtbar genug,
euch zu sehn?

Mantelaug, Mandelaug, kamst
durch alle die Wände,
erklimmst
dieses Pult,
rollst, was dort liegt, wieder auf—

Zehn Blindenstäbe,
feurig, gerade, frei,
entschweben dem eben
geborenen Zeichen,

steh
über ihm.

Wir sind es noch immer.

SIGHT THREADS SENSE THREADS, from
nightbile knitted
behind time:

who
is invisible enough
to see you?

Mantle-eye, almondeye, you came
through all the walls,
climb
on this desk,
roll, what lies there, up again—

Ten blindstaffs,
fiery, straight, free,
float from the just
born sign,

stand
above it.

It is still us.

EIN DRÖHNEN: es ist
die Wahrheit selbst
unter die Menschen
getreten,
mitten ins
Metapherngestöber.

A ROAR: it is
truth itself
stepped among
mankind,
right into the
metaphor-flurry.

IRRENNÄPFE, vergammelte
Tiefen.

Wär ich——

Nun ja, wär ich
die—wohin gebogene?—
Esche draußen,

ich wüßte dich zu begleiten,
leuchtendes Graugericht mit
dem dich durchwachsenden, schnell
herunterzuwürgenden Bild
und demeng-
gezogenen, flackernden
Denkkreis um euch
beide.

LUNATIC-BOWLS, rotten
depths.

Were I—

Well, yes, were I
the—whither bent?—
ashtree outside,

I would know how to accompany you,
shining graydish with the
quickly to be gulped
down image marbling you,
and the tightly
drawn, flickering
thought-circle around you
both.

LICHTENBERGS ZWÖLF mit dem Tischtuch
ererbte Mundtücher—ein
Planetengruß an
die Sprachtürme rings
in der totzuschweigenden Zeichen-
Zone.

Sein[37]

—kein Himmel ist, keine
Erde, und beider
Gedächtnis gelöscht
bis auf den einen
eschengläubigen Blauspecht—,

sein
vom Stadtwall gepflückter
weißer Komet.

Eine Stimmritze, ihn
zu bewahren,
im All.

LICHTENBERG'S TWELVE with the tablecloth
inherited napkins—a
planet-greeting to
the language-towers everywhere
in the to-be-silenced-to-death sign-
zone.

Being

—no heaven is, no
earth, and the
memory of both extinguished
but for the one
ashtree-believing nuthatch—,

his
from the city-ramparts gathered
white comet.

A voice-rift, to
preserve him, in
the universe.

Das Rotverlorene eines
Gedanken-
fadens. Die laut-
gewordenen Klagen
darüber, die Klage
darunter—wessen
Laut?

Damit—frag nicht,
wo—
wär ich fast—
sag nicht wo, wann, wieder.

The redlorn of a
thought-
thread. The bur-
geoned laments
about it, the lament
below it—whose
sound?

With it—don't ask
where—
I nearly—
don't say where, when, again.

GIVE THE WORD

Ins Hirn gehaun—halb? zu drei Vierteln?—,
gibst du, genächtet, die Parolen—diese:

"Tatarenpfeile".
                "Kunstbrei".
                        "Atem".

Es kommen alle, keiner fehlt und keine.
(Sipheten und Probyllen sind dabei.)

Es kommt ein Mensch.

Weltapfelgroß die Träne neben dir,
durchrauscht, durchfahren
von Antwort,
           Antwort,
                    Antwort.
Durcheist—von wem?

"Passiert", sagst du,
                "passiert",
                    "passiert".

GIVE THE WORD

Cut to the brains—half? three quarters?—,
you give, benighted, the passwords—these:

"Tatararrows."
                    "Artpap."
                                "Breath."

All are coming, no one's missing.
(Siphets and probyls are among them.)

A man comes.

Worldapplesize, the teardrop beside you,
swept through, crossed
by answer,
              answer,
                        answer.
Iced-through—by whom?

"Pass," you say,
              "pass,"
                        "pass."

Der stille Aussatz löst sich dir vom Gaumen
und fächelt deiner Zunge Licht zu,

                              Licht.

The quiet lepra peels off your palate
and fans light to your tongue,
                              light.

VOM ANBLICK DER ANSELM, abends,
durchs Unvergitterte, das
mich umringt,

versprach ich mir Waffen.

Vom Anblick der Waffen—Hände,
vom Anblick der Hände—die längst
vom flachen, scharfen
Kiesel geschriebene Zeile

—Welle, du
trugst ihn her, schliffst ihn zu,
gabst dich, Un-
verlierbare, drein,
Ufersand, nimmst,
nimmst auf,
Strandhafer, weh
das Deine hinzu—,

die Zeile, die Zeile,
die wir umschlungen durchschwimmmen,
zweimal in jedem Jahrtausend,
all den Gesang in den Fingern,

FROM BEHOLDING THE BLACKBIRDS, evenings,
through the unbarred, that
surrounds me,

I promised myself weapons.

From beholding the weapons—hands,
from beholding the hands—the long ago
by the sharp, flat
pebble written line

—Wave, you
carried it hither, honed it,
gave yourself, un-
losable, up,
shoresand, you take,
take in,
sea-oats, blow
yours along—,

the line, the line,
through which we swim, entwined,
twice each millennium,
all that singing at the fingers,

den auch die durch uns lebendige,
herrlich-undeutbare
Flut uns nicht glaubt.

that even the through us living,
magnificent-unexplainable
flood does not believe us.

V

GROSSE, GLÜHENDE WÖLBUNG
mit dem sich
hinaus- und hinweg-
wühlenden Schwarzgestirn-Schwarm:

der verkieselten Stirn eines Widders
brenn ich dies Bild ein, zwischen
die Hörner, darin,
im Gesang der Windungen, das
Mark der geronnenen
Herzmeere schwillt.

Wo-
gegen
rennt er nicht an?

Die Welt is fort, ich muß dich tragen.

GREAT, GLOWING VAULT
with the
outward- and away-
burrowing black-constellation swarm:

into the silicified forehead of a ram
I burn this image, between
the horns, therein,
in the singing of the coils, the
marrow of the curdled
heartseas swells.

What
doesn't he
butt against?

The world is gone, I have to carry you.

SCHIEFERÄUGIGE, von
der schreitenden Gegenschrift am
Tag nach der Blendung erreicht.

Lesbare Blutklumpen-Botin,
herübergestorben, trotz allem,
von wissenden Stacheldrahtschwingen
über die unverrückbare
Tausendmauer getragen.

Du hier, du: verlebendigt
vom Hauch der im frei-
geschaufelten Lungengeäst
hängengebliebenen
Namen.

Zu
Entziffernde du.

Mit dir,
auf der Stimmbänderbrücke, im
Großen Dazwischen,
nachtüber.

Mit Herztönen beschossen,
von allen Weltkanzeln her.

SLATE-EYED ONE, reached
by the striding counterscript the
day after the blinding.

Readable bloodclot-messenger,
hither-died, despite all,
carried by knowing barbedwirewings
over the undisplaceable
thousandwall.

You here, you: quickened
by the breath of the
names
caught in the free-
shovelled lungbranches.

To-
be-deciphered you.

With you,
on the vocalcords' bridge, in the
great Inbetween,
nightover.

Shot at with hearttones,
from all the world-pulpits.

SCHLICKENDE, dann
krautige Stille der Ufer.

Die eine Schleuse noch. Am
Warzenturm, mit
Brackigem übergossen,
mündest du ein.

Vor dir, in
den rudernden Riesensporangien,
sichelt, als keuchten dort Worte,
ein Glanz.

Oozy, then
weedy silence of the shores.

The one sluice yet. At
the warttower, doused
with brackish,
you empty into.

Before you, in
the rowing giant sporangia,
as if words panted there, a
lustre sickles.

Du, DAS mit dem hell-
sehenden Hochschlaf von
der Lippe genommene Haar:
durchs Goldöhr der
zurechtgesungenen Aschen-
nadel gefädelt.

Du, der mit dem Einen
Licht aus dem Hals
gerissene Knoten:
durchstoßen von Nadel und Haar,
unterwegs, unterwegs.

Eure Umschwünge, immerzu, um
die sieben-
fingrige Kußhand hinterm
Glück.

You, the hair taken from
the lip with the bright-
seeing highsleep:
threaded through the goldeye
of the sung-aright ash-
needle.

You, the knot torn out
of the throat with
the One Light:
run through by needle and hair,
underway, underway.

Your reversals, incessantly, round
the seven-
fingered kisshand behind
happiness.

DER MIT HIMMELN GEHEIZTE
Feuerriß durch die Welt.

Die Wer da?-Rufe
in seinem Innern:

durch dich hier hindurch
auf den Schild
der Ewigen Wanze gespiegelt,
umschnüffelt von Falsch und Verstört,

die unendliche Schleife ziehend, trotzdem,
die schiffbar bleibt für die un-
getreidelte Antwort.

THE WITH HEAVENS HEATED
firefissure through the world.

The Who's there?-calls
inside it:

mirror-cast through you here
onto the shield
of the Eternal Bug,
sniffed around by False and Bewildered,

looping the unending loop, nevertheless,
which stays navigable for the un-
towed answer.

DUNSTBÄNDER-, SPRUCHBÄNDER-AUFSTAND,
röter als rot,
während der großen
Frostschübe, auf
schlitternden Eisbuckeln, vor
Robbenvölkern.

Der durch dich hindurch-
gehämmerte Strahl,
der hier schreibt,
röter als rot.

Mit seinen Worten
dich aus der Hirnschale schälen, hier,
verscharrter Oktober.

Mit dir das Gold prägen, jetzt,
wenns heraustirbt.

Mit dir den Bändern beistehn.

Mit dir das glasharte Flugblatt vertäuen
am lesenden Blutpoller, den
die Erde durch diesen
Stiefpol hinausstieß.

VAPORBAND-, BANDEROLE-UPRISING,
redder than red,
during the great
frostthrusts, on
sliding ice-bucklings, before
seal nations.

The beam hammered all
the way through you,
that writes here,
redder than red.

With its words
to shuck you out of the brainshell, here,
hastily buried October.

With you to coin the gold, now,
when it dies out of.

With you to assist the banderoles.

With you to moor the glasshard leaflet
to the bloodbollard, that
the earth pushed out
through this step-pole.

RUH AUS IN DEINEN WUNDEN,
durchblubbert und umpaust.

Das Runde, klein, das Feste:
aus den Blicknischen kommts
gerollt, nahebei,
in keinerlei Tuch.

(Das hat
—Perle, so schwer
wars durch dich—,
das hat sich den Salzstrauch ertaucht,
drüben, im Zweimeer.)

Ohne Licht rollts, ohne
Farbe—du
stich die Elfenbeinnadel hindurch
—wer weiß nicht,
daß der getigerte Stein, der dich ansprang,
an ihr zerklang?—,
und so—wohin fiel die Erde?—
laß es sich drehen zeitauf,
mit zehn Nagelmonden im Schlepptau,
in Schlangennähe, bei Gelbflut,
quasistellar.

Rest in your wounds,
blubbered out, lulled.

The round, small, the firm:
from the gazeniches it comes
rolling, nearby,
into no kind of cloth.

(It has
—Pearl, it was
so difficult through you—,
it has, diving, won the saltbush,
over there, in the Twosea.)

Without light it rolls, without
color—you,
stick the ivory needle through it
—who doesn't know
that the tigered stone, that jumped you,
rang out on it?—,
and so—whither fell earth?—
let it turn time-up,
with ten nailmoons on the towrope,
in serpent-nearness, at yellow-flood,
quasistellar.

VI

Einmal,
da hörte ich ihn,
da wusch er die Welt,
ungesehn, nachtlang,
wirklich.

Eins und Unendlich,
vernichtet,
ichten,

Licht war. Rettung.

ONCE
I did hear him,
he did wash the world,
unseen, nightlong,
real.

One and unending,
annihilated,
I'ed.

Light was. Salvation.

THE COMMENTARIES

The numbers of this section refer to the footnotes in the German text of the poems. Besides their obvious function of trying to provide some minimal information concerning difficulties both in the original poems and in the translations, these commentaries will point out the kind of complexities an in-depth reading, hermeneutical or other, will have to contend with. Obviously what is proposed here are only a few exempla that should not be mistaken for an annotated translation of any completeness. These minimalia function more as a map of ignorance than as a showcase for knowledges regarding Celan's late poems.

1   The first cycle of *Breathturn* was published under the title *Atemkristall* with eight etchings by Gisèle Celan-Lestrange in a bibliophile edition from Brunidor, Paris, 1965.

2   This poem, and the next one, are among the few that have so far been studied according to their various manuscript stages by one of the scholars involved in publishing the critical Celan edition [Bücher, R. (1986). Erfahrenes Sprechen—Leseversuch an Celan-Entwürfen. *Argumentum e Silentio*. Berlin, de Gruyter.] In the first ms. version the second section (after the colon) of this poem read: "(...) ich komme mit sieben / Blättern vom Sieben- / stamm." (I come with seven / leaves from the seven- / trunk.) After analyzing the Jewish / kabbalistic component of the early version, including the relation of the seven-armed candelabra, the menorah, to the world tree, Bücher writes: "The poem should still be understood entirely with an eye to this image's genealogical heritage, in the sense of the original image of the 'seven-trunk.' " [here "Stamm" means both tree-trunk and tribe]. Bücher goes on to suggest that a straightforward reading of the early version "would lead to a very abstract sense of 'heritage,' which must also be seen, in its narrowest context, as a very concrete Judaism," concluding that it is specifically "this abstractness which is caught in the published version of the poem, and transposed into the image of a concrete life experience."

3   This cycle opens and closes with one of Celan's strongest and most cherished images: snow. See, among others, Hans-Michel Speier's essay on the posthumous volume *Schneepart*. "Schnee," and the associated ice and glacier cosmos, traverse *Breathturn*. See, for example, the much commented lines (page 106):

> Tiefimschnee,
>> Iefimnee,
>>> I - i - e.

4   The earliest version of this poem begins:

> Traumgeätzt,
> wirft das durchwanderte Brotland den Berg auf.
>
> (Dream-etched
> the wandered-through breadland casts up the mountain.)

A hand-emendation inserts "schlaflos," which then requires in the following version of the poem the logical change from "traumgeätzt" into its opposite, "von Ungeträumten geätzt." Bürger's comment on this is worth quoting *in extenso*:

> This will to paradox, which corresponds with the often observed paradoxes of Celan's work, here shows itself most clearly as determining and putting into motion the poetic fixing-process. Only insofar as a logical paradox seems to be cleared up, namely the contradiction between sleeplessness and dream-reality, does an extremely effective pictorial paradox arise—in the reality and effectiveness of an absence, the "undreamt." In this paradox, the "undreamt" is yet again tendered in the poem as dream-reality, and enters into a new contradiction with "sleeplessly" in the second line.

5   "Gebräch" is a hunting term and refers to the ground uprooted by wild boars. Unable to find the exact corresponding term, I have preferred to translate—albeit by an overly abstract word—the core term of the German word, which is the verb "brechen," to break. Lynch

and Jakowsky have tried to keep the hunting image alive, and give the line as "PATHS in the boar-tusked shadowland," which sounds not only contrived, though vaguely Celanian, but also introduces two terms, "boar" and "land" that are not in Celan's text. [Celan, P. (1985). 65 Poems. Translated by Brian Lynch and Peter Jankowsky. Dublin, Raven Arts Press.]

By translating "wühlen" in the next stanza as "root up" I hope that some sense of the hunting / animal terminology is brought back in.

6 Georg-Michael Schulz provides an excellent analysis of this poem in an essay in the Celan-Jahrbuch 2 ("'Sterblichkeitsbeflissen'. Zu Paul Celans Gedicht 'Wege im Schatten-Gebräch.'" CJB. 2: 29–36.) According to him, the poem is based on a very specific iconic image: a figure one can find in Jewish cemeteries on a number of grave stones... a figure of two hands in the gesture of blessing." He goes on to quote a description of how the hands have to be held during the blessing ritual which lies at the origin of the grave inscription. It is this mudra-like figure that creates the "four-finger-furrow":

> ...the finger thus, with pinkie touching ring-finger, and the likewise linked middle and index fingers propped [sic], these (for their part) by both thumbs, so that five interstices ensue—two each opening up above; the middle ones, between the thumbs down below.

7 This and the following poem have been analyzed in detail in relation to Celan's use of dream-language [Böschenstein-Schäfer, R. (1987). Traum und Sprache in der Dichtung Paul Celans. Argumentum e Silentio. Berlin, Walter de Gruyter]. Böschenstein-Schäfer suggests that Celan, like many survivors of terrorist regimes and despite his attraction to Surrealism, is wary of dreams and afraid of invasion or betrayal of / by that most private area, the unconscious. He has two ways of defending himself against this:

> Of these the first is the concentration on *awakening*, the second, the replacement of the *structures of dream speech* in the poetic. In the place of the dream image the poet thematizes the attempt to produce, through the recollection of the dream,

contact with the unconscious. "Shaft," "gorge" and "suction pipe" are all variants of the vertical, which especially in the volumes *Breathturn*, *Threadsuns* and *Lightduress* characterize the way dream elements enter into consciousness.

In these poems one can also hear a Lacanian theme: the unconscious / the dream is / as language. It is more than likely that during the sixties in Paris Celan was aware of, and probably read, Lacan.

8 A possible reference to the "Gate of Horn" which according to Homer leads to the true dreams (*Odyssey* 19, 562–569).

9 "Morgen-Lot" is one of a number of paranomastic constructions that pose insurmountable difficulties for the translator. They are based on common German expressions— in this case "Morgenrot"— which do not carry over into the translation, but which in the German poem the new word forces one to also read / hear. In this specific case the translation also loses a further connotation, that of the biblical figure Lot who was led by the angels from the condemned city at dawn—"als die Morgenröte aufging."

10 Hartmut Steinecke has written a sharp-tongued essay comparing the various analyses this poem (and it is one of the most discussed of Celan's poems) has been subjected to. [Steinecke, H. (1987). Lieder…jenseits der Menschen? *Psalm und Hawdalah. Zum Werk Paul Celans.* Bern, Peter Lang.]

11 "Light-tone" or, possibly, "light-pitch" are literal translations of "Lichtton," if one considers the word as a Celanian composite. The German word is however also a technical term in filmography where it refers to the process of "sound-on-film" in which sound is inscribed as variations of light values on film.

12 Celan owned a copy of the pre-Socratic fragments which contains the following orphic text, consisting of directions on how to enter Hades [Böschenstein-Schäfer, R. (1987). Traum und Sprache in der Dichtung Paul Celans. *Argumentum e Silentio*. Berlin, Walter de Gruyter, p. 234]. It is reproduced from: Freeman K. (1983). Ancilla to

the pre-Socratic Philosphers: A Complete Translation of the Fragments in Diels' "Fragmente der Vorsokratiker." Cambridge, Harvard University Press, p.5:

> You will find a spring on the left of the halls of Hades, and beside it a white cypress growing. Do not even go near this spring. And you will find another, from the Lake of Memory, flowing forth with cold water…. And they themselves will give you to drink from the divine spring….

Concerning the "Schlangenwagen," Böschenstein-Schäfer suggests the following reading:

> …the image of the serpentcoach: in this are knotted the image of Medea of Kolchis, fleeing in despair in a chariot drawn by dragons, and of the muse's chariot, even as Pindar or Empedocles hoped to mount it…(p. 234)

13 For a fascinating reading of this poem, see K. Manger, "Paul Celans poetische Geographie." *Psalm und Hawdalah: Zum Werk Paul Celans.* Bern, Peter Lang (1987). Hans-Georg Gadamer's reading of the same poem goes wrong, as James K. Lyon has shown, because he misunderstood the vocabulary: the first three words are geological terms, with "Harnischstriemen" referring to striae, i.e. striations "on rock surfaces that are visible where monolithic blocks have been scraped against each other during large-scale volcanic upheavals." I prefer to use another geological term, "slickensides," a more interesting English word, which my geological dictionary defines as "fine parallel scratches or grooves on a fault surface that have been produced by the movement of the rocks on either side of the fault." "Faltenachsen" signify "the direction of the thrust when the earth's strata are folded by volcanic activity to form rises and depressions." [Lyon, J. K. (1974). "Paul Celan's Language of Stone: The Geology of the Poetic Landscape." CG. (3/4): 298–317 p. 304]

14 If "Durchstichpunkte" belongs to the same vocabulary as the two previous words, i.e. geology, then it refers to "a technical term in flood control for cutting through sharp curves in a meandering river,

i.e. a means of altering the landscape by rechannelling the river."
But—cf. Lyon—another meaning is also possible: "[it] can also refer
to the points left in a chart or map which is copied by means of
pinpoints."

15 For a discussion of Celan's use of "poles," see E. Hünnecke's essay
"'Hoffnung auf ein menschliches Heute und Morgen.' Zur
Wirklichkeit in der Dichtung Paul Celans" in the Celan Jahrbuch 1
pp. 149–150. In the posthumous volume *Zeitgehöft*, the poles reemerge
in a poem that seems worth quoting here in full (in my translation),
as it clarifies Celan's understanding of these "poles," which are closely
linked to his other, better-known geographical image, the merid-
ians:

> THE POLES
> are in us,
> insurmountable
> while awake,
> we sleep across, to the Gate
> of Mercy,
>
> I lose you to you, that
> is my snowcomfort,
>
> say that Jerusalem is,
>
> say it, as if I was this
> your Whiteness,
> as if you were
> mine,
>
> as if without us we could be we
>
> I leaf you open, forever,
>
> you pray, you lay
> us free.

16 The rose, flower image/metaphor is a central concept throughout much of Celan's work. cf. the volume *Die Niemandrose*. It becomes rarer in the later volumes and appears only three times (twice as a composite and once as the flower name) from *Breathturn* on. The present composite, "Kluftrose," seems most likely to derive from "Windrose" or compass rose.

17 This poem, written for his wife Gisèle in 1965, has been examined by many commentators. For one of the most complete analyses, see Lyon, J. K. (1987). "Ganz und gar nicht hermetisch": Zum "richtigen" Lesen von Paul Celans Lyrik. *Psalm und Hawdalah. Zum Werk Paul Celans*. Bern, Peter Lang. pp. 185–189.

18 Celan's neologism "Mein- / Gedicht" is based analogically on the German word "Meineid," a false oath, perjury.

19 "Findling" in German has two distinct meanings: (1) as a variant of "Findelkind" it means a foundling (child); (2) as a geological term it translates as "glacial erratic" and refers (according to my dictionary) to "a large piece of rock, or boulder, that has been carried by ice for some distance and has then come to rest where the ice has melted."

20 The biblical Esther was an orphan who, married to the non-Jewish King Ahasuerus, managed to thwart a plot to kill all the Jews.

21 Untranslatable pun combining "Schlüsselburg," an infamous prison town in Russia where during the days of the Czar many revolutionaries were executed, and "Schlüsselblumen," primroses or cowslips, a traditional symbol of spring. Renate Böschenstein-Schäfer also suggests that the number twenty could point to the twenty-one members of the Narodnaja-Volna-Movement, who were imprisoned at the town in 1884 and nearly all died.

22 "Gebetsriemen" literally translated means "prayer-belt"; the term is however a specific object in Judaism (called "phylactery" in English) where it refers to:

Either of two small leather boxes, each containing strips of parchment inscribed with quotations from the Hebrew scriptures. One is strapped to the forehead, the other to the left arm by observant Jewish men during morning worship, except on Sabbath and holidays.

A second, archaic meaning of "phylactery" is amulet, reminder. Although the technical, Greek-derived term "phylactery" may seem odd or even overdetermine the German compound, the context here clearly points to the Jewish cult object, something an English neologism such as "prayerbelt" would not.

23 "Blütig," a Celan neologism that mixes "blutig" (bloody, bleeding, etc.) with "blühen, blüte, etc." i.e. the word convolute around flower /flowering/blossom. The translator's neologism "bloodsoming" tries, however clumsily, to render this double load.

24 The last line poses major difficulties for the translation. "Versandend" has the sense of being progressively mired in sand, to "silt up"; "Verhoffst," repeating the "ver-" particle in a typical Celanian way seems at first semantically to reduplicate the meaning of "versandend" suggesting the progressive loss of hope. But the verb "verhoffen" is in fact a technical hunting term usually used in reference to deer and meaning "to stand quietly and scent the wind." This double meaning of loss of hope and yet of a still active listening to the world gets lost in translation. But given the negative connotation of "bogged in," translating the active, hunting sense of "verhoffst" with "scent" (as in "to scent danger") seems the least unfaithful possibility.

25 "Laufkatze Leben" is an untranslatable compound; Celan obviously wants the reader to hear "Katze" (cat) and "Lauf" (run) as descriptive of "Leben," but the word "Laufkatze," especially given the poem's harbor-geography, is also the technical apparatus called in English a "trolley" or "trolley hoist." So far I have been unable to find an English equivalent that would render this meaning-complex in a satisfactory manner. Paratactic juxtaposition of both meanings seems the only way, combined with the female pronoun "she" rather than the expected "it."

26 The play on "spiegeln"—to mirror, to reflect—and on the name Till Eulenspiegel—the saxon "Narr," clear in German—does not translate well. The name has been translated as "Owlglass" in English versions of the tales and this seems to be here the best—or least deleterious—way of proceeding.

27 According to Bernd Witte, this poem, and the one preceding it, commemorate a meeting with the poet Ingeborg Bachmann and include references to Bachmann's poem "Prag Jänner 64," whose lines "Unter den berstenden Blöcken / meines, auch meines Flusses / kam das befreite Wasser hervor," (Under the bursting blocks / of my, yes even my river / the freed water appeared) are echoed in the previous poem's lines: "there the rods dipped royally before our eye, / water came, water...." [Witte, B. (1986). Der zyklische Charakter der *Niemandsrose* von Paul Celan. *Argumentum e Silentio*. Berlin, de Gruyter]
    According to Pöggeler's more hermeneutical reading, the "wir" concerns essentially "die Begegnung des Dichters mit seinem Du" ("the encounter of the poet with his You") [Pöggeler, O. *Spur des Wortes*. München, Verlag Larl Alber (1986), p. 366]

28 Witte: "So baut 'der halbe Tod,' der Tod-im-Text, sich ins 'Wohin', auf den offenen Ausgang des Gedichtes zu." ("Thus 'half death,' death-in-the-text, builds itself into the 'whereto,' toward the open exit / conclusion of the poem.") Witte reads the poem as a programmatic metapoem, which seems quite possible. One can however also find another layer which links it to the "Todesfuge" and the fate of the Jewish people. [Witte, B. (1987). Eine Poetik des Todes. Celans Baudelaire-Übertragung und das Motiv des Todes in seinem Spätwerk. *Datum und Zitat bei Paul Celan*. Bern, Peter Lang.]

29 Possibly a reference to the legend of the thirty-six Just Ones. Pöggeler asks:

> Are the stairs those of the Hradčany, and are those holy figures meant who stand on the Karlsbrücke, something like a thirty-figure group? One should rather think of the 36 just men, who vouch their own lives to help the persecuted, who perhaps outweigh the extermination machinery of evil in the scales of

time, to which in any case they don't leave the last word. [*Spur des Wortes*, p. 354]

30 Bernd Witte reads the "Goldmacher-Nein" as a reference to the "Alchimistengasse," situated close to the Hradčany in Prague, and the street in which Kafka lived when he wrote the "Landarzterzählungen." [Witte, p. 239]

31 Compare in the early volume *Mohn und Gedächtnis* the poem "Spät und tief" which contains the line: "Ihr mahlt in den Mühlen des Todes das weiße Mehl der Verheißung." ("In the mills of death you grind the white flower of Promise.) Compare also the poem "Out of angel-matter" in *Threadsuns*.

32 The complexly convoluted syntax of this one-sentence stanza is irreproducable in English. In the first version of the translation it read:

> The from you also star-
> eyed loafer melancholy
> hears of it.

A seond version tried to clarify the English:

> The—because of you also star-
> eyed—loafer Melancholy
> learns of it.

But the problem is in fact one of meaning; I am unable to clarify the German meaning to my satisfaction, and am therefore at a loss in relation to the translation. The decision in this—and a few similar cases—has been to remain with the most literal translation possible.

33 "Schwirrhölzer" is an ethnological term referring to the cult object known in English as a "bullroarer," used in Africa and Australia. But the German word lets the reader also hear the two basic words that make up the compound, namely "wood" and "whirring." I have tried to retain some of that whirr / whizz sound by translating the indeterminate "fahren" as "whizz".

34 Concerning "-blütig" cf note 23 above.

35 It is possible to read the dyptic "Solve" and "Coagula" as programmatic of the poetics of late Celan: a dissolving and a reorganization of both reality and language. See also next note.

36 The title as well as the previous poem indicate an alchemical theme—and possible references to the Christian esoteric mysticism of the Rosy Cross. But the "Rosa" here also refers to Rosa Luxembourg through the "Rumanian buffaloes." In relation to Rosa Luxembourg, compare the poem "Du liegst" in the posthumous volume *Schneepart*.

Other connections with the theme of "solve et coagula" can be found, according to Pöggeler—who seems well aware of Celan's reading—in Hoffmanthal's "Andreas", where the following formulation occurs: "Das 'Ergon', sagt die Fama, 'ist die Heiligung des inneren Menschen, die Goldmacherkunst ist das Parergon'—solve et coagula." ("The 'Ergon,' says the Fama, 'is the sanctification of the inner man, the art of making gold is the parergon'— solve et coagula.") [Pöggeler, Spur *des Wortes*, p.306]

Compare also the poem "In Prag" for alchemical themes. On the image of the rose in Celan's poems, compare: Winkler, M. (1972). "On Paul Celan's Rose Images." Neophilologus. LVI (1): 72–78.

37 The next stanza, standing between dashes, functions as an interjection, at the end of which "sein" is repeated and the sentence completed. But this interjection allows for the possibility of reading the first "Sein" not as the possessive pronoun it first was—or at least seems to be— and becomes again later ("sein...weißer Komet") but as the verbal noun "Sein," Being.

[*My thanks to Benjamin Friedlander and Andy Schmitz for help in translating the German citations in these commentaries.*]

Paul Celan

Born in Czernowitz, the capital of the Bukovina (now part of the Ukraine and Rumania), in 1920, Paul Celan was raised in a Jewish family that insisted both on the young Paul receiving the best secular education—with the mother inculcating her love of the German language and culture—and knowledge of his Jewish roots. By 1939 he started to write and that year began to study Romance literature. In 1940 Soviet troops occupied his home town, only to be replaced by Rumanian and German Nazi troops the next year. Celan had to work in forced labor camps, where, in the fall of 1942, he learned that his father, physically broken by the slave labor he was subjected to, had been killed by the ss. Later that winter the news reached him that his mother too had been shot. These killings, especially that of his mother, were to remain the core experience of his life. Released a year later, he remained at the now Sovietized University of Czernowitz until he left the Bukovina for good in April 1945. He lived in Bucharest until December 1947, when he clandestinely crossed over to Vienna, which he left in 1948 to settle in Paris, the city that was to be his home until his suicide by drowning in the Seine in April 1970.

Among Celan's major writings are *Mohn und Gedächtnis* (1952), *Sprachgitter* (1959), *Die Niemandsrose* (1963), *Atemwende* (1967), *Fadensonnen* (1968), and *Lichtzwang* (1970). Three posthumous volumes of late poetry have appeared, as well as a volume of collected prose.

Pierre Joris, the translator, left Luxembourg at eighteen and has since lived in the United States, Great Britain, North Africa, and France. He has published over twenty books of poetry, among them, *Winnetou Old, Turbulence,* and *Breccia: Selected Poems 1974–1986,* as well as several anthologies and numerous volumes of translations, both into English and into French, the most recent being Maurice Blanchot's *The Unavowable Community* and Edmond Jabès' *From the Desert to the Book.* He is currently collaborating with Jerome Rothenberg on a two volume anthology of 20th Century Avant-Garde writings, *Poems for the Millennium: A California Press Book of Modern & Postmodern Poetry,* to be published in 1995 and 1997. Rothenberg's and Joris' previous collaboration *pppppp: Selected Writings of Kurt Schwitters* was awarded the 1994 P E N Center U S A West Literary Award for Translation. Joris is a professor at the State University of New York-Albany.

SUN & MOON CLASSICS

This publication was made possible, in part, through an operational grant from the Andrew W. Mellon Foundation and through contributions from the following individuals and organizations:

Tom Ahern (Foster, Rhode Island)
Charles Altieri (Seattle, Washington)
John Arden (Galway, Ireland)
Paul Auster (Brooklyn, New York)
Jesse Huntley Ausubel (New York, New York)
Luigi Ballerini (Los Angeles, California)
Dennis Barone (West Hartford, Connecticut)
Jonathan Baumbach (Brooklyn, New York)
Roberto Bedoya (Los Angeles, California)
Guy Bennett (Los Angeles, California)
Bill Berkson (Bolinas, California)
Steve Benson (Berkeley, California)
Charles Bernstein and Susan Bee (New York, New York)
Dorothy Bilik (Silver Spring, Maryland)
Alain Bosquet (Paris, France)
In Memoriam: John Cage
In Memoriam: Camilo José Cela
Bill Corbett (Boston, Massachusetts)
Robert Crosson (Los Angeles, California)
Tina Darragh and P. Inman (Greenbelt, Maryland)
Fielding Dawson (New York, New York)
Christopher Dewdney (Toronto, Canada)
Larry Deyah (New York, New York)
Arkadii Dragomoschenko (St. Petersburg, Russia)
George Economou (Norman, Oklahoma)
Richard Elman (Stony Brook, New York)
Kenward Elmslie (Calais, Vermont)
Elaine Equi and Jerome Sala (New York, New York)
Lawrence Ferlinghetti (San Francisco, California)
Richard Foreman (New York, New York)
Howard N. Fox (Los Angeles, California)
Jerry Fox (Aventura, Florida)
In Memoriam: Rose Fox
Melvyn Freilicher (San Diego, California)
Miro Gavran (Zagreb, Croatia)
Allen Ginsberg (New York, New York)

Peter Glassgold (Brooklyn, New York)
Barbara Guest (Berkeley, California)
Perla and Amiram V. Karney (Bel Air, California)
Václav Havel (Prague, The Czech Republic)
Lyn Hejinian (Berkeley, California)
Fanny Howe (La Jolla, California)
Harold Jaffe (San Diego, California)
Ira S. Jaffe (Albuquerque, New Mexico)
Ruth Prawer Jhabvala (New York, New York)
Pierre Joris (Albany, New York)
Alex Katz (New York, New York)
Tom LaFarge (New York, New York)
Mary Jane Lafferty (Los Angeles, California)
Michael Lally (Santa Monica, California)
Norman Lavers (Jonesboro, Arkansas)
Jerome Lawrence (Malibu, California)
Stacey Levine (Seattle, Washington)
Herbert Lust (Greenwich, Connecticut)
Norman MacAffee (New York, New York)
Rosemary Macchiavelli (Washington, DC)
In Memoriam: Mary McCarthy
Harry Mulisch (Amsterdam, The Netherlands)
Iris Murdoch (Oxford, England)
Martin Nakell (Los Angeles, California)
In Memoriam: bpNichol
NORLA (Norwegian Literature Abroad) (Oslo, Norway)
Claes Oldenburg (New York, New York)
Toby Olson (Philadelphia, Pennsylvania)
Maggie O'Sullivan (Hebden Bridge, England)
Rochelle Owens (Norman, Oklahoma)
Bart Parker (Providence, Rhode Island)
Marjorie and Joseph Perloff (Pacific Palisades, California)
Dennis Phillips (Los Angeles, California)
Carl Rakosi (San Francisco, California)
Tom Raworth (Cambridge, England)
David Reed (New York, New York)
Ishmael Reed (Oakland, California)
Tom Roberdeau (Los Angeles, California)
Janet Rodney (Santa Fe, New Mexico)
Joe Ross (Washington, DC)
Jerome and Diane Rothenberg (Encinitas, California)
Edward Ruscha (Los Angeles, California)

If you would like to be a contributor to this series, please send your tax-deductible contribution to The Contemporary Arts Educational Project, Inc., a non-profit corporation, 6026 Wilshire Boulevard, Los Angeles, California 90036.

SUN & MOON CLASSICS